History
TODAY

Ancient Voices
Learning from Pompeii

Ann Sloane

DayOne

© Day One Publications 2013
First printed 2013

ISBN 978–1–84625–398–0

British Library Cataloguing in Publication Data available

Published by Day One Publications
Ryelands Road, Leominster, HR6 8NZ
☎ 01568 613 740 FAX 01568 611 473
email—sales@dayone.co.uk
web site—www.dayone.co.uk
North America—email—usasales@dayone.co.uk

Cover design by Wayne McMaster
Printed by TJ International

Appreciations

Ann Sloane has given us a brilliant account of the destruction of Pompeii, Herculaneum and other places near to Vesuvius.

We are taken back to Roman Cities in the first century AD to a time when the New Testament was being written, and through the pages of this book you can walk through ancient streets, alive with people, noise and many different odours, some more exotic than others.

Just like Sodom and Gomorrah of the Old Testament, you can appreciate something of the awful nature of destruction as it unfolded, and learn many powerful and searching lessons so relevant for life in the twenty-first century.

Clive Anderson, Alton, Hampshire

Dedication

For my children: Rebecca and Nathan.

Contents

I n Campania (a beautiful region of Italy), near the town of Naples, is Pompeii, a city which for over 1,500 years lay hidden from the world. Surprisingly, because it is still hidden by the town that has grown up around it, there is no sense of the amazing sight that awaits you beyond the walled entrance. After the coach pulls into the car park, the local guide walks you to the entrance. The odd fallen Roman pillar is the only indication of what lies within. Upon entering through the original Marina Gate and being taken up to the forum you can't help but get a sense of wonder at its sheer size and the amount of history still contained within what is, to all intents and purposes, a time capsule.

With the hot sun bearing down it is easy to close your eyes and let your imagination run riot. The hustle and bustle of the tourists and the shouting of the guide suddenly become the sounds of the long-gone townsfolk. The city is no longer in ruins, but a vibrant cosmopolitan community full of grand architecture. Walking away from the forum and down the quieter back streets, away from the tourists, you come across ruins of the shops, public baths and the amphitheatre. The remarkable ruins reveal what life was like in a Roman city during the first century AD when the New Testament was being written.

Now, with eyes open again, you are struck by the very cause of Pompeii's demise. Mount Vesuvius looms over all and casts its shadow upon the now silent town while threatening the very existence of the new town that surrounds it. You get back on the coach for the short ride to the mountain itself, and then, after walking up the dusty zigzag path to its summit, you gaze down upon the gaping maw that is the crater. Only small clouds of smoke betray the menace beneath. Silent for the moment, it is difficult to imagine how dangerous it is.

Another day's journey takes you to Herculaneum, a former seaside resort where wealthy Romans liked to go for their holidays and the most well-known of Vesuvius' other victims. Although smaller than Pompeii, she is perhaps better preserved. Entombed within the modern-day city of

1 Pompeii: Although overgrown with grass, the oldest surviving amphitheatre in the world is still majestic.

Ercolano, entry is gained by walking down a purpose-built ramp. Although now far inland, one can still get a sense of how it might once have looked in the days when its sumptuous villas would have overlooked the sea. Vesuvius is not visible from Herculaneum, its view obstructed by the walls of solidified lava which encircle it. Perched crazily on the edge of the precipice formed by these walls are the modern houses of today.

Two other towns faced the same fate as Herculaneum and Pompeii, but these are not so well known: Stabiae, which was also a seaside resort, catering to the rich and famous with its positively palatial villas, and Oplontis, with its villas, baths, agricultural storerooms and land.

But in order that we may best understand the terrible events that happened in AD 79 we will take a look at the nation that gave Pompeii and Herculaneum their culture, religion and art—The Roman Empire.

The Rise of the Roman Empire

'The Most High God is sovereign over the kingdoms of men and sets over them anyone he wishes.'   Daniel 5:21

2   Statue of the Capitoline Wolf (Lupa Capitolina) suckling the abandoned twins Romulus and Remus.

The Caesars

Legend has it that Rome was founded on 21 April 753 BC by Romulus, who killed his twin brother Remus in a battle over where the city should be built and what name to give it. However, for the sake of convenience we will skip forward about 600 years, for the real Roman Empire began with the coming of the Caesars.

Chapter 1

'Veni, Vidi, Vici' (I came, I saw, I conquered)   Julius Caesar

Julius Caesar was born in 100 BC, supposedly by caesarean section, although historians think this unlikely. Said to be tall and handsome with dark, piercing eyes, he led an extremely adventurous life. At the age of 25 he was kidnapped by pirates and while waiting for the ransom to be paid, it was said he exercised, joked and even treated his captors like his servants. Eventually, when the ransom had been paid, he set about capturing the pirates and crucifying every last one of them.

He was ambitious and worked his way up the political and military ladder, conquering Gaul and, after one failed attempt, Britain in 54 BC.

In 48 BC, a three-times-married 52-year-old Julius met the 22-year-old Queen of Egypt, Cleopatra. Legend has it that she wrapped herself in a carpet and was in this fashion delivered to Caesar. In 47 BC Julius left Egypt for Rome and was later followed by Cleopatra and their son Caesarion. In 44 BC he was named 'Dictator Peretuus' (dictator for life), but he did not hold that position for long. Within a year, as the result of a conspiracy by over 40 senators, he was assassinated in a brutal attack on the fifteenth (ides) of March at the Theatre of Pompey. Cleopatra fled back to Egypt claiming Caesarion to be Julius Caesar's legal heir to Rome and a god. Cleopatra then took Mark Antony as her lover. He had been sent to take over the administration of the Eastern provinces.

The legal heir to Julius Caesar was Gaius Octavius Thurinus Augustus, who now regarded Mark Antony and Cleopatra as a threat and set out to eliminate them. Eventually, after several battles, Mark Antony committed suicide by falling on his sword. Cleopatra also took her own life which, according to legend, she accomplished by allowing herself to be bitten by a poisonous asp. Following this the young Caesarion, just 17 years old, was quickly executed, finally leaving the field clear for Gauis Octavius Thurinus Augustus who was pronounced 'Caesar Augustus' in 27 BC—the first Caesar.

A time of peace

Augustus, known before becoming Caesar as Octavius, is considered to be one of the greatest Caesars; he even has a month named after him. He brought some stability and a time of peace to Rome, ending civil wars and fortifying its existing boundaries while pushing into new territories. He also introduced a regular army and a stronger infrastructure with decent roads—vital for transporting goods as well as troops. He even took it upon himself to restore the old religion of worshipping the gods, believing it was all a part of what made Rome great. This period was known as the Pax Romana.

Although Emperors and leaders of Rome had always had their bodyguards, Augustus decided he needed an elite group of soldiers to protect him. They were to be the best of the best and totally loyal to the Emperor. They were called the praetorian guard (praetorian meaning 'tent' belonging to the leader of the army). Originally consisting of 4,500 men they were exempt from usual army duty and did not have to fight in battle unless specifically requested to do so by the Emperor or if the Emperor himself participated in battle. Originally Augustus had the idea that they would also act as a kind of police force keeping law and order—even wearing 'plain clothes' inside the palace. However, as time went on the praetorian guard became a law unto themselves.

The new Empire covered most of Europe, parts of Asia and Africa and, of course, Israel. It was during Augustus' reign that a young girl by the name of Mary, who was living in Nazareth in Israel, received an angelic message that she would be the mother of the Saviour of the world and that she was to give him the name Jesus. Heavily pregnant, Mary and her husband Joseph would be forced to travel to Joseph's home town of Bethlehem because of a decree issued by Augustus that everyone who fell under Roman jurisdiction would need to be registered, probably for taxation reasons. Caesar would use this census for his own purposes, but God would use it to ensure that biblical prophecy would come to pass:

'But you, Bethlehem Ephrathah, though you are small among the clans of Judah, out of you will come for me one who will be ruler over Israel, whose origins are from of old, from ancient times' (Micah 5:2). Had this not been part of God's plan it is very likely that Mary and Joseph would have stayed in Nazareth.

On 19 August AD 14 Caesar Augustus died aged 76. There is still some debate as to whether he died of natural causes or whether his death was 'hastened' by his wife Livia and his heir Tiberius.

Alea jacta est (the die is cast)

Born Tiberius Julius Caesar Augustus on 16 November 42 BC, he was not Augustus' original choice of heir, but due to the death of all other candidates (whether by natural causes or not), he became Emperor Tiberius on 17 September AD 14. Intelligent and successful politically and militarily, he was also given to bouts of depression. His reign is a bit of an enigma to historians. Although he began well, he was prone to trust the wrong people, particularly his advisor Lucius Aelius Sejanus. Around AD 26 Tiberius retired from public life to the Isle of Capri, where, in his palace called the Villa Jovis (villa of Jupiter), it was said he indulged himself in licentious acts and sank even further into depression. Believing in his own self-importance, Tiberius denied himself nothing, killing anyone who disagreed or upset him in any way, usually by throwing them off a thousand-foot cliff.

With Sejanus left in charge, a reign of terror began, during which many of the noble men and women were imprisoned or executed for trivial misdemeanours and their property confiscated. Sejanus was stopped only when Tiberius had him executed on grounds of treason—it seems that Sejanus had become a little too big for his boots.

In Rome at that time there was a large Jewish community which had been established in the city for many years. They had sometimes been harshly treated, but both Julius Caesar and Emperor Augustus had been favourable towards them. However, in AD 16 the Jews were sent into exile or conscripted into the army because three Jewish men had defrauded Fulvia, an aristocratic Roman woman. Fulvia had been attracted to Judaism and had been asked by the three to give them gold and purple linen for the temple in Jerusalem—unfortunately they sold the linen and gold and used the money for themselves.

It was during Emperor Tiberius' reign that Pontius Pilate was appointed Governor of Judea between AD 26 and AD 36. Known for his military expertise rather than his diplomatic tact, he was ordered by Emperor Tiberius to respect the culture of Judea and to rule in conjunction with the Jewish authorities. However, the historian Josephus states that Pilate provoked the Jews by insisting that the Roman Imperial standard be carried into Jerusalem. He was also believed to have siphoned off Jewish revenue to build an aqueduct and massacred all members of a Jewish revolt who tried to sabotage the project. It was Pilate who presided at the trial of Jesus washing his hands of an innocent's blood but agreeing to Jesus' death nonetheless. The death of this 'rebellious nobody' would be the fulfilment of God's promise to send a saviour who would restore peace between himself and man, but to Pilate he was just a fly in the ointment, whose death would bring satisfaction to an angry mob.

Interestingly it was a Roman soldier, a centurion, who made perhaps the most profound statement, as he stood at the foot of the cross supervising the crucifixion and death of Jesus. This rugged, hardened, pagan soldier watched as Jesus was flogged, beaten, abused and then finally dragged out and hung on a cross to die. The soldier would have been used to watching prisoners die in this way, but as the events unfolded he realised that this time it was different. So different that he declared Jesus to be 'a righteous man' (Luke 23:47) and 'the Son of God' (Mark 15:39).

Emperor Tiberius died on 16 March AD 37 aged 77. Again, no one knows for sure if he died of natural causes or whether, as legend has it, he was smothered by a praetorian guard when his heir Gaius Caesar Augustus Germanicus took Tiberius' signature ring off prematurely, having assumed Tiberius to be dead, and pronounced himself Emperor.

Mad, bad and dangerous to know

Gaius Caesar Augustus Germanicus is perhaps better known as Caligula. Caligula means 'little boots'—a name he was given by the army, as he would often accompany his father Germanicus, dressing up in armour and boots. At the age of 25 he became Emperor and was said to have been weak in health and prone to fits. If the populace of the Roman Empire thought things were bad under Emperor Tiberius, things were about to get a lot worse. For four years Caligula indulged in cruel, extravagant and sexually immoral acts, declaring himself a god and demanding worship from all citizens of Rome. Historians say that a lot of what we know of Caligula is based on hearsay or myth as there are very few written records left of his reign.

True or not, the actions attributed to him are appalling. It is said that during a gladiatorial game he ordered an entire section of the audience to be thrown to wild animals simply for his amusement. He gave himself over to every kind of sexually depraved act, forcing many of the rich noble born women into prostitution in what can only be described as a brothel created within the palace. Extravagant in his spending it was said that, having used up all his own personal money, he would execute the rich and elite of Rome and claim their properties and monies as his own. He committed incest with at least two of his sisters, later banishing them from Rome. He made Incitatus, his favourite horse, a consul and priest. In AD 40 he even declared that a statue of himself should be erected in front of the Temple of Jerusalem so that Jews would be forced to worship him—a direct violation of the command given by God 'You shall have no other gods before me' (Exodus 20:3). The then governor of Syria,

Petronius, realised the seriousness of the situation and used delaying tactics for nearly a year.

It is now wondered whether Caligula was suffering from a form of bipolar disorder (also called manic depression). Certainly, he did not have a particularly happy childhood; his father died of a strange illness (or was he poisoned by Tiberius?), his mother committed suicide and two of his brothers were executed by Tiberius. He also spent seven years on the Isle of Capri watching the aged Emperor Tiberius indulging himself in every whim, all of which may well have affected Caligula deeply.

Whatever his mental state, it was finally resolved on 24 January AD 41, when three praetorian guards, led by Cassius Chaerea, again took matters into their own hands and assassinated Caligula in an underground passage beneath his own palace. Cassius Chaerea had been a centurion under Caligula's father and had been humiliated by him. Strangely, although Caligula was feared and abhorred by many of the rich and powerful he was adored by the 'average Joe' in the street who demanded justice for the murdered Emperor. The best thing about his reign was that, at nearly four years, it seems to have been mercifully short.

An unlikely candidate

It is believed that, having murdered the despotic Caligula, the praetorian guard searched the palace and found Tiberius Claudius Drusus hiding behind a curtain and proclaimed him Emperor. Later in order to ingratiate himself with the citizens of Rome, Claudius would hunt down and execute all those that had taken part in the assassination of Caligula.

Claudius was Tiberius' nephew and Caligula's uncle. Rejected by his own family because of a limp and a speech impediment, he was an unlikely candidate for emperor. Indeed, although appointed a Consul by Caligula, it is thought he was at the palace only as an object of ridicule. The Senate initially did not accept him as emperor.

Not known as a military man he nevertheless accomplished the successful re-invasion of Britain in AD 43. Sending his troops ahead Claudius joined them later in the campaign bringing with him 38 war elephants and heavy artillery, his arrival in Britain heralded the defeat of 11 British tribes within just 16 days. Emperor Claudius returned back to Rome to a hero's welcome. On the home front he was married to Messallina, his third wife, with whom he had two children Octavia and Britannicus. However after 10 years of marriage Messallina declared herself to be married to the Consul Silius and attempted to assassinate Claudius—the pair were executed.

In AD 44, following the death of Herod Antipas, Judea also came under direct Roman rule.

In AD 49 Claudius married his niece Agrippina the Younger, sister to Caligula, who had returned from exile. Agrippina had a son of her own, Lucius Domitius Ahenobarbus, who was older than Britannicus and Claudius was persuaded to adopt Lucius as his own. Upon adoption he changed his name to Nero Claudius Drusus Germanicus Caesar. Agrippina was an aggressive opponent eliminating any who got in her way, while promoting the advancement of Nero and reducing Claudius to just a figurehead. Perhaps we should not feel too sorry for Claudius— he was also known as bloodthirsty, cruel, quick to anger and overly fond of both gladiatorial combat and executions. He was also responsible for the death of many senators.

During AD 49 there was yet another ejection of the Jews from Rome, this time because the Jews were making constant disturbances. The historian Suetonius claims that the instigator of the trouble was 'Chrestus'—there is an ongoing debate as to whether this is a reference to Christ or merely some troublesome unknown character. This does, however, tie in with Acts 18:2, where Paul goes to Corinth: 'There he met a Jew named Aquilla, a native of Pontus, who had recently come from Italy with his wife Priscilla, because Claudius had ordered all the Jews to leave Rome'. What is certain is that the rise of the early Christian church was causing problems for Rome.

On 13 October AD 54 Claudius was attending a feast when he died, possibly poisoned by Agrippina. As Britannicus was no longer recognised as Claudius' heir, Nero became Emperor.

Power corrupts; absolute power corrupts absolutely

At the tender age of 17, it seemed at first that Emperor Nero would follow in Augustus' footsteps and herald in a time of peace and prosperity, but it was not to be. It is thought that his mother Agrippina desired to rule through or jointly with him—historians have even discovered coins with both their images upon them—but Nero preferred the counsel of his advisers Seneca and Burrus. To ensure there would be no opposition, less than a year after becoming Emperor, Nero poisoned his step-brother Britannicus claiming that the 13-year-old boy had died following an epileptic fit, a condition that did run in the family. Not content with that, in AD 59 Nero arranged an 'accident' for his mother. When that failed he ordered the execution of Agrippina on the grounds of treason.

Nero's greatest desire was to be known as a musician, poet, singer and actor, something the Romans found abhorrent as this put their Emperor on a level with prostitutes. It was likely that he had no talent: the

3 A coin showing Nero and his mother Agrippina; it was very rare for a ruling Emperor and a woman to both appear on the same side of a coin.

historian Suetonius reports that his voice was 'naturally neither loud nor clear'[1], but this did not stop him from holding endless recitals during which it was forbidden to leave. With the gates locked and barred, it was said that the recitals lasted so long that women gave birth and men feigned death in order that they might be carried out for burial. Nero was also an eager athlete and although not necessarily a good one, he nonetheless won every event he took part in—no one dared to beat him. Historians tell us that on one occasion he fell from his chariot during a race and that the other competitors prudently waited for him to re-mount and win.

In Britain during AD 60–61 a red headed Iceni woman by the name of Boudicca became a problem for the Romans. Leading her armies on a rampage of destruction she burnt to the ground parts of Londinium (London) and Verulamium (St Albans), killing about 70,000 people, not all of whom were Romans! Nero briefly toyed with the idea of withdrawing from Britain, but despite the problems and his troops being heavily outnumbered, Boudicca was defeated by the Roman governor Suetonius.

In AD 62 Nero divorced and banished his wife Octavia, Claudius' daughter, whom he would later execute, and married his mistress, ex-slave Poppaea. Poppaea did not fare much better; three years later it is said that Nero kicked a pregnant Poppaea to death. Anyone who opposed him or got in his way was executed. A group of senators who plotted to kill Nero were rounded up, branded, scourged and then killed. He married for a third time to Statilia Messalina, after making her husband commit suicide, and although not much is known of her she was fortunate enough to outlive Nero. It should be noted that historians generally tend to doubt accounts of the life of Nero, as they were usually written by people with biased views of the man, but there are good grounds to accept them.

On 5 February AD 62 the region of Campania was hit by an earthquake with Pompeii at its epicentre. Although many homes and buildings were destroyed and people displaced Nero sends no aid to the beleaguered city.

Who's to blame?

In AD 64 a great fire broke out in Rome and speculation as to its cause has raged on ever since. Popular belief has it that Nero himself started the fire to make room for his ambitious building projects, not least of which was his own palace, the Domus Aurea (golden house), so called because of its gold-covered walls. The blame, Nero ensured, fell on a new religious group that were causing trouble for him and the rest of the Roman Empire – the Christians. Michael Bentley, in his book 'Living for Christ in a Pagan World', says 'stories began to circulate about them. It was said that they worshiped a criminal—one who had been tried before a Roman proconsul, who had been found guilty and had been executed by the traitor's death of crucifixion'[2]. Fear and hatred of this strange religious group, who worshipped only one god and refused to sacrifice to the Emperor, was growing.

There had obviously been persecution of the Christians going right back to the time of the stoning of Stephen, as recorded in the Bible (Acts 7:54–60), but Nero brought in a whole new level of cruelty. He used their deaths as a form of entertainment, as reported by historian Tacitus: 'Mockery of every sort was added to their deaths. Covered with the skins of beasts, they were torn by dogs and perished, or were nailed to crosses, or were doomed to the flames and burnt, to serve as a nightly illumination, when daylight had expired.'[3] It is also believed that during this time of great persecution both the apostles Peter and Paul met their ends in Rome.

The apostle Paul, who was a Roman citizen, had appealed to plead his cause before the Emperor Nero when he was arrested in Jerusalem following a near riot by the Jews. Before leaving for Rome, Paul had the opportunity to preach before King Agrippa II and his sister Bernice, with whom Agrippa was having an incestuous affair. King Agrippa was the great grandson of Herod the Great, who at the time of Jesus' birth had ordered the death of all baby boys in an effort to eliminate the Messiah, and he was the son of King Agrippa I who had arrested the apostle Peter and beheaded the apostle James (Acts 12:2). Also in the audience were Felix, Procurator of Judea and his wife Drusilla (sister to the previously mentioned Bernice). Felix had kept Paul as his prisoner for almost two years as a favour to the Jews and had probably had many a talk with him.

During his trip to Rome, Paul faced all manner of hardships, only one of which was being shipwrecked. Finally reaching his destination, he was placed under house arrest where he continued to preach the gospel under the watchful eye of the praetorian guard. Paul tells us in his letter to the Philippians that 'As a result, it has become clear throughout the whole palace guard and to everyone else that I am in chains for Christ' (1:13). That some of Nero's own staff had become Christians is evident when Paul finishes his letter to the same Philippians by saying 'All the saints send you greetings, especially those who belong to Caesar's household' (4:22).

While the persecution of the Christians continued, the Jewish populace rose up in AD 66 against the Roman Procurator Gessius Florus, retaking control of Jerusalem, killing the garrison and taking control of various other areas of Judea. An army of 30,000 was sent as a response under the control of Cestius Gallus, who managed to encircle the Jews for eight days in Jerusalem. Then, for reasons known only to himself, he withdrew his troops back to Beth-Horon, where they were attacked and defeated by the rejuvenated rebels. In response Emperor Nero sent in the 'big guns', despatching General Titus Flavius Sabinus Vespasianus with 60,000 men. They successfully secured the Galilee area, slowly recapturing territory as they went until, by AD 68, the rebels were isolated in Jerusalem.

While all this was going on Nero decided to go to Greece and participate in a competition for musicians. He won many awards while he was there, including competitions in which he did not take part! In his absence, the remaining senators began to pass a motion to remove him from power. When Nero returned to Rome the ever-determined and powerful praetorian guards, together with the Gallic and Spanish legions, gave Nero no choice but to flee from Rome and finally to commit suicide on 9 June AD 68. The people rejoiced: after 13 years they were finally rid of Nero. But they wanted more and the senate passed what was called a damnation memoriae, (literally 'condemnation of memory'), meaning that the person must not be remembered.

The year of four emperors

There then followed a time of civil war in Rome with the rise and fall of three emperors: Servius Sulpicius Galba, Marcus Salvius Otho and Aulus Vitellius—all of whom met untimely ends. In July AD 69 Vespasianus was proclaimed emperor by his legions and, leaving his son Titus to take command in Israel, he returned to Rome now as Emperor Vespasian.

Vespasian had three main objectives during his reign: to restore Rome's finances after Nero's wastefulness, to restore discipline, and to ensure the succession of his son Titus. He succeeded in all three. It was Vespasian who ordered the building of the famous Colosseum, and began a restoration and rebuilding project, repairing damage that had been caused during the fire of AD 62. He also funded projects in the beleaguered towns of Pompeii and Herculaneum, still devastated after the earthquake.

He had one wife by the name of Flavia Domitilla who died before he became emperor and whom historians believe he genuinely loved. After her death he lived with his mistress Caenis, who it is said had considerable influence over him. It is believed he lived a relatively simple life and died a normal death at the age of 69 on 23 June AD 79 following a

4 A scene from the Titus Arch showing the temple treasures and Israelite slaves being brought back to Rome.

short illness. The historian Tacitus says of him 'he was the first man to improve after becoming emperor'.4

The destroyer of Jerusalem

Vespasian's son Titus Flavius Vespasian now became Emperor Titus and seems to have at first been unpopular with both the people and the senate due to his ruthlessness, for the continuance of taxes and for his ongoing affair with Bernice, the previously mentioned daughter of Herod Agrippa I, sister and lover to Herod Agrippa II. Intelligent, strong and a fierce warrior, it was during his father Vespasian's reign that Titus finally ended the siege of Jerusalem by slaughtering thousands of Jews. Of those that survived, thousands were taken either into slavery or sent to the mines in Egypt. It was Titus who destroyed the Temple, leaving only one wall of it standing, which became known as the Western or Wailing Wall. The Titus Arch in Rome depicts his victory as he parades through the streets displaying the new slaves and the treasures of the Temple. This led to the cessation of the daily sacrifices and the Jewish high priesthood, just as Jesus predicted: 'Not one stone here will be left on another; every one will be thrown down!' (Mark 13:2).

Once Titus became Emperor it appears that the spin doctors took over and his image began to be depicted in a more positive light. Titus arranged that building work on the Colosseum was finished and, at its opening, showed that he too could be extravagant by funding lavish games to entertain the populace.

It was just two months into the reign of Emperor Titus when the events surrounding the eruption of Mount Vesuvius took place. Titus' reign, although short at just over two years, was dogged by catastrophe; the eruption of Vesuvius was followed by a fire in Rome and an outbreak of plague, but during all of this his popularity increased. Finally and suddenly at the age of 41 he died, whether of natural causes or killed by his successor and brother Domitian we will never know.

Notes

1 http://ancienthistory.about.com/library/bl/bl_nero_suetonius.htm—section XX

2 **Bentley, Michael,** *Living for Christ in a Pagan World* (Co. Durham, England: Evangelical Press, 1990), p. 33.

3 http://www.livius.org/cg-cm/christianity/tacitus.html

4 http://www.bbc.co.uk/history/historic_figures/vespasian.shtml

The cities and the people

[quote]'Pompeii was the miniature of the civilization of that age … It was a toy, a plaything, a showbox, in which the gods seemed pleased to keep the representation of the great monarchy of the earth, and which they afterwards hid from time to give to the wonder of posterity—the moral of the maxim, that under the sun there is nothing new.'   *Last Days of Pompeii* by Baron Edward George Bulwer-Lytton[1]

5 The forum with Vesuvius dominating the background.

According to legend, when the mighty Hercules was returning from Spain he stopped in the area of Campania and founded two cities: Herculaneum, which he modestly named after himself, and Pompeii from the word 'pompa' meaning procession, alluding to his triumphal march home. (Other traditions say it is the Oscan word for five—'pompe' – suggesting that there were originally five hamlets in that area.) When we think of Italy it is easy to assume that everyone was Roman, but until the Empire really took off, only its capital Rome was truly Roman. Many of the outlying regions were inhabited by tribes, and much of the early history of Pompeii, as far as we know, is dominated by successive tribes from the region of Campania. According to the historian Strabo, the Etruscans were the first to establish a small fishing village at Herculaneum on the high ground, giving them a good strategic position; and Pompeii, which they built on an ancient volcanic lava ridge. Inter-tribal wars meant that Pompeii was held subsequently by the Pelasgians (who were Greek) and later still by another Oscan-speaking tribe called the Samnites. After many years and an unsuccessful Italic tribal uprising against Rome, they were finally defeated and Campania was annexed in 89 BC.

As an interesting aside it is worth mentioning that in 73 BC a revolt was organised by Spartacus, an outlawed freeborn who was sold into slavery and trained at the gladiatorial school of Batiatus in Capua. Escaping with about 80 other gladiators, they made their way to Campania and camped within the crater of Vesuvius, where they were joined by other rural slaves. The senate sent Claudis Glaber with 3000 raw recruits to recapture the slaves believing they had them trapped within Vesuvius, but Spartacus led his men down the other side of the mountain using grape vines and fell upon the soldiers from the rear, routing them.

The slave revolt was finally defeated by Marcus Licinius Crassus, who crucified 6,000 of them along the Appian Way. Whether Spartacus was one of them or whether he died on the battlefield no one knows.

A fortified city

Due to the unrest caused by the slave revolt against Rome, pillaging by the rebel slaves and a war against Rome itself, Pompeii became a fortified city which had twelve defensive towers built into its surrounding wall. There were also eight gates or entry points into the city; the Marine Gate being used today as the main access point for tourists. Others include the Vesuvius Gate, which led to a road heading inland around Mount Vesuvius; the Herculaneum Gate—which, unsurprisingly, led to Herculaneum; and the Stabiae Gate.

Originally located on the coast, Pompeii is believed to have been a port city but due to successive eruptions it now lies 2km/1.25 miles inland. It is located 11km/7 miles southeast of Vesuvius and covers an area of approximately 157 acres (0.245 square miles) and was thought to have had a population of between 8,000 and 10,000 inhabitants at the time of the eruption.

Inside the walls was a criss-cross geometric grid system of straight roads, based on the ideas of Greek architect Hippodamus. The main roads were called the Via Stabina (Stabiae Road), the Via delle Terme (Baths Street), Via della Fortuna (Fortune Street), the Via di Nola (Nola Road) and the Via dell'Abbondanza (Abundance Street). From these ran the many side streets. The main roads quite often had a pavement or sidewalk area for pedestrians and stepping stones for crossing when the roads were flooded or when horses had been through! There were also pedestrian-only zones which were cordoned off from traffic by stone bollards.

Every modern convenience

The fresh water for Pompeii was provided by an aqueduct system which fed into a roofed reservoir (Castellum Aquae) before dividing into three large lead pipes which ran under the pavements and which in turn, working solely on gravity, fed the 43 public fountains which were situated on nearly every street corner. Leading off these three main pipes was a network of smaller pipes which provided water to shops, the public baths and even some of the more wealthy privately owned houses. There was also an elaborate underground drainage system which took rainwater and overflow from the fountains back into the system. The water from the latrines was directed into a separate underground cistern.

House and home

Houses or villas, just like today, varied in age, style and size from the very modest to the extravagant. Nero's tragic wife Poppaea was said to have owned a rather palatial villa on the outskirts of Pompeii at Oplontis, with over 100 rooms and a private 60-metre swimming pool. But unlike today's houses, the owners' homes were very much a part of their business lives. In his book *Houses and Society in Pompeii and Herculaneum*, Andrew Wallace-Hadrill states 'Post-industrial society has become accustomed to a divorce between home and place of work. Status is generated at work not home, so the home becomes endowed with a "privacy" alien to the Roman.'[2]

Wealthy Romans divided their houses into two parts: the public and the private, the public being large reception rooms with fantastic wall coverings evoking images of the forum or the Theatre, with columns or even vaulted ceilings. Then there were the slightly less public rooms, such as the dining area where only those invited were allowed to enter. These were still lavishly decorated with mythical stories or gods and goddesses. Next there were the private: the bedrooms or cubiculum with their almost wallpaper-like decorations. Finally, there were the slave areas, including the kitchen, where decoration was basic as it was unlikely that the visitor would enter these parts of the house.

Usually rectangular in shape, entrance was made through a short corridor into an atrium, a large central opening with rooms leading off, upstairs and down. In the middle of the atrium there would sometimes be an impluvium or small pool, which would catch rainwater as there was no roof above it. Off the atrium would sometimes be more reception rooms, with another corridor to the bedroom or kitchen and slave area. Alternatively it would lead towards the garden or peristylum, located at the back or centre of the house. These would often be lavishly decorated with fountains and flowerbeds and would, to all intents and purposes, serve as another reception room. Everything was done to impress the owner's business associates.

Famous statesman and orator Cicero had a summer house at Pompeii and took great pains to decorate and fill it to create just the right impression; many of its murals were subsequently removed during excavation and taken to the Museum in Naples. One particular colour is very dominant in many of the murals at Pompeii: it is a shade of deep dark

6 House of the Vetti looking through the atrium to the peristylum in the background. You can see the impluvium (rainwater pool) in the foreground.

red which became known as 'Pompeian Red' when the paintings were first uncovered. It became very popular in the Victorian era for decorating English walls. However, it has recently been discovered that Pompeian Red is more likely to have originally been yellow, which turned red when mixed with the gasses given off in the eruption.[3]

Local government

Although the forum was the main spiritual, political and social hub of the town, local government was conducted at the basilica. Legal pronouncements were made by two elected duumviri iure dicinduo (magistrates, also known as duumvir), who kept office for four years. Under these were four aediles who were responsible for the maintenance of streets, supervision of the markets and policing; i.e. the day to day running of a city. Below them was a multitude of scribes and assistants. Neither the duumvir or aediles were paid for their services and, as they were expected to pay for the wages of scribes, etc., and host gladiatorial displays, they tended to be from the more wealthy families.

Interestingly, Emperor Caligula became a duumvir of Pompeii twice. Mary Beard in her book *Pompeii: The Life of a Roman Town* writes 'How exactly would Caligula's duumvirate have been arranged? And where would the initiative have come from: the imperial palace or Pompeii itself? One theory is that by inserting an emperor or prince into the local government, even in an honorary capacity, the central authorities in Rome were attempting to gain some control of affairs in the town. It was, in other words, a punishment or a rescue bid after some crisis in the town's management. Hard as it is to imagine the mad Caligula ever being more of a help than a hindrance, maybe even a nominal imperial presence would make scrutiny and central government intervention easier.'[4]

The population was well catered for by its numerous shops, fast food outlets, cafes, taverns and bakeries. On the entertainment front there were two theatres, the larger of which held up to 5,000 people and was thought to have presented the latest play in comedy or tragedy. There were fan clubs for the most popular actors and many residents would have pictures of their favourite plays painted on their home walls, similar to the manner in which posters are sometimes used today. The smaller theatre, known as the Odeon, held 1,500 spectators and is likely to have hosted poetry readings or perhaps singing recitals.

The word vomitorium originates from the Roman theatres, it is not, as originally and mistakenly quoted, a room where those that have stuffed themselves silly can go and be sick and come back to fill themselves again, although apparently this did happen. It in fact means the exits from the theatre where people are, if you like, vomited from the theatre!

Hero worship

There was also a large amphitheatre which could seat 20,000 spectators and was the place to go to see gladiatorial or animal displays, a little like going to see a football match today (though probably a little more lethal!). There were different styles of gladiator from the chariot racer to the cavalryman, from the heavily armoured to the lightly armoured with just a net and trident to fight with. Gladiators quite often had a large female following or 'fan base' who would avidly follow their hero's progress—it was not unusual for a gladiator to be mobbed by his adoring female fans, reminiscent of pop stars today. However, despite their popularity gladiators were in fact slaves—well fed and well trained but owned by others and whose job was to fight (sometimes, but not always to the death) for the entertainment of the spectators.

Unfortunately, in AD 59, during the reign of Nero, the amphitheatre was home to a serious disturbance, as described by historian Tacitus: 'there arose from a trifling beginning a terrible bloodbath among the inhabitants of the colonies of Nuceria and Pompeii at a gladiatorial show

7 Fresco showing the ad 59 riot in the amphitheatre.

given by Livineius Regulus, whose expulsion from the senate I have recorded previously. Inter-town rivalry led to abuse, then stone throwing, then the drawing of weapons. The Pompeians in whose town the show was being given came off the better. Therefore many of the Nucerians were carried to Rome having lost limbs, and many were bereaved of parents and children.'[5] The ultimate consequence was that the senate in Rome passed a ten-year ban on any similar gathering in Pompeii.

Next to the amphitheatre was the palestra (gym) which had a large sports ground and a swimming pool and was used as a training ground for the young men of Pompeii.

Bring your own towel!

There were also the baths—the Romans loved the baths and they were a crucial feature in Roman life. Pompeii had at least five public baths: the Stabian, the largest and oldest; the forum; the suburban, which has only quite recently been excavated; the Amphitheatre, which was reburied after its excavation; and the central, so new that it had not been opened to the public before the eruption in AD 79. Men and women would have had separate sections within the baths or different times of the day when they could attend.

All the baths operated in the same way; people would enter through the changing rooms (apodyterium), where they would deposit their clothes in alcoves which acted as lockers. Then they would move on to the tepidarium (warm room), where underfloor heating known as hypocausts would heat the room to a pleasant temperature and the customer would begin to sweat. After that they would move on to the caldarium (hot room) where temperatures would soar. Sometimes it got a bit too hot and the customers would complain. The historian Seneca wrote 'The temperature that men have recently made fashionable is as great as a conflagration, to such an extent that a slave convicted for a criminal act could be boiled alive. It appears to me that today there is no difference between the "bath is hot" and the "bath is on fire"'.[6] But if they felt that it wasn't hot enough there was also a kind of sauna area known as the laconicum. Then it was back to the tepidarium to be oiled, scraped and massaged—there was no soap in those days and patrons were expected to provide their own oil and towels!

Finally came the frigidarium (cold room) for a plunge in the freezing cold water—very invigorating. Afterwards customers could relax by having a nice warm or cold drink, play games or talk business—it wasn't just a way of getting clean, but also a noisy social event and something to be enjoyed by all. Just how 'clean' the people were after visiting the baths is open to question as no filtration system has yet been discovered and, as far as we know, chlorination was not known about in those days. It is more than likely that they were drained, as the beautifully preserved Roman baths in Bath, England have been, but it is equally likely that they were drained only occasionally.

The darker side of life

Unfortunately, there was also the inevitable seedy side to Roman life, namely the brothels. The females and males that worked in these establishments were quite often foreign slaves, but occasionally a person of high birth would register. Even though the Roman attitude to sex was very liberal the people involved were still thought of as second class citizens, with those working in these 'trades' not allowed to vote, hold office or marry a free-born Roman. Although there is only one definitive brothel in Pompeii, the lupanar, it is thought there were at least ten brothels in the city, though some estimates put the number as high as 35, a figure viewed with scepticism these days. Some were decorated in what we would see as extremely lewd and pornographic pictures while others were just basic. The lupanar itself is an extremely dismal place with uncomfortable stone carved beds in what can only be described as prison cells rather than rooms.

Too many gods

Romans worshipped a multitude of different gods and there have been several temples excavated so far. They include those dedicated to the Greek god Apollo, the Roman god Jupiter, the Emperor god Augustus and even the Egyptian goddess Isis. The people also had little 'house shrines' in which they would worship their favourite god—one of the most popular at Pompeii was Bacchus, the god of wine and good living.

There was also evidence of trade with many other cultures, including India: an ivory statuette of the goddess Lakshmi having been found in a house on the Via dell' Abbondanza. There is also evidence of trade with Jews, some of whom were very probably resident in Pompeii.

The question of whether there were any Christians in Pompeii is a matter still under discussion. The apostle Paul certainly had been in the region, as it says in the book of Acts 'the following day we reached Puteoli. There we found some brothers who invited us to spend a week with them' (Acts 28:13–14). Puteoli (now Pozzuoli) was in the region of Naples and the fact that he was met by brethren shows the probability of a Christian fellowship in that area. Also the great persecution during Nero's reign would have caused Christians to flee to the countryside, thus spreading the gospel. Senator Pliny the Younger, an eyewitness to the AD 79 eruption, spoke of Christianity as a plague, saying 'The contagion of this superstition has spread not only to the cities but to the villages and farms.'7 Pliny would take this even further during the reign of Emperor Trajan (AD 52–117), and would go on to torture and execute Christians, stating 'Meanwhile, in the case of those who were denounced to me as Christians, I have observed the following procedure: I interrogated these as to whether they were Christians; those who confessed I interrogated a second and a third time, threatening them with punishment; those who persisted I ordered executed.'8

There was a hotly debated inscription, supposedly discovered on wall of a house (possibly the house of Publius Paquius Proculus I–7.1) off the Via dell' Abbondanza which shows a word square (a Rotas-Sator Square) which contains 25 letters which can be rearranged to spell Pater Noster AO. Pater Noster means Our Father and AO could be translated as Alpha and Omega. There was said to be another Rotas Square etched on a column near the amphitheatre, unfortunately all traces of these two word squares seem to have disappeared. At Herculaneum on the upper floor of the 'Bicentenary House' there is a deeply etched mark on the plaster wall in the shape of a cross. This was originally held up as evidence that Christianity had reached the city, but is now thought to be where a bracket for a cupboard once sat. Although the debate rages on, it is extremely likely that Christianity was known and heard about in the cities, and very possibly there were Christians in Pompeii and Herculaneum but because of fear of persecution it would have been kept quiet.

The quick and the dead

Just outside the city walls was the necropolis, or cemetery. Today we tend to keep the dead well away from the living, but in AD 79 it was customary for tombs to line the main road leading up to cities as well as a dedicated area just for the small mausoleums or elaborate tombs. It was the practise to cremate the dead, their ashes being kept in urns inside the tombs or their remains placed under a Herm, or tiled marker (like a headstone) which was usually carved in the shape of a head. Grave goods such as coins or jewellery were also buried with the ashes. There also appears to have been no class distinction in death, graves having been found to commemorate both the rich and the poor, Roman citizen and freedman and even slave, men, women and children.

Nightlife

Although very little is known of what went on in Pompeii, or indeed any Roman town, after nightfall, we can assume that not everything came to an abrupt halt when it became dark. Of course they did not enjoy the luxury that we have today of electric street lamps, but they did have an abundance of oil lamps, many of which have been recovered, although the illumination afforded by these would have been very poor. Many shops had wooden screens so that shopkeepers could 'shut up shop', but the brothels and taverns would have continued to ply their wares. It is also possible that deliveries to local shops may have continued into the night. Mary Beard paints a very vivid picture when she writes: 'As well as the howling dogs, the carousing of the "late drinkers", the whistling and joking of the sign painters at their jobs, we have to imagine the sounds of the rumbling carts, the jingling of the bells, the scraping of iron-clad wheels against the kerb or the stepping stones. Literally, a city that never slept—and was never quiet.'9

Diet and health

What of the people themselves, what did they like to eat? Studies of human excrement in a recently uncovered cesspit at Herculaneum have revealed the diet of the locals as wide and varied and also enjoyed by rich and poor alike. They ate olives, grapes, figs and pears not unlike us today but they were also partial to the odd dormouse and occasional sea urchin too.

With scientific advancement has come the ability to study the skeletal remains of the residents of Pompeii, opening up a whole new dimension on life in Roman times. The average age of the citizens ranged from 26 to 40, but at least one foetus has been discovered within its mother's skeleton (in the house of Julius Polybius) and some skeletons are put at over 60 years of age. The average height was 5 feet 5 inches (1.66 metres) for men and just over 5 feet (1.53 metres) for women.

It has also been discovered that they suffered from all kinds of diseases from tooth decay to arthritis, and surprisingly at least 11 per cent suffered from Spina Bifida (a deformation of the spinal cord caused during development). A recent project at what is believed to be an agricultural depot in Oplontis has revealed a startling piece of information on the health of the locals. Hidden in the cellar of a converted villa over fifty skeletons were discovered huddled together. Amongst them were twins, aged between 10 and 12 years old, suffering from what is believed to be congenital syphilis. Passed through the placenta from an infected mother, it is a sexually transmitted disease and to the children infected it would be severe and debilitating. Even today it is considered life-threatening. This discovery is startling because syphilis is believed to be a fairly recent (fifteenth century) disease, but it also shows that even in ancient times where so-called sexual liberty was rife; consequences would have to be faced.[10]

The family

Family life was ruled by the father 'patria potestas', which meant that he literally had the power of life and death over his family. When a new child was born the baby was laid at his feet; if he picked it up it was allowed to live, if he ignored the child it was put outside by a slave, 'exposed' and left to die. Even in Roman England evidence has been uncovered of infanticide; in a sewer beneath what was thought to be a brothel, over 50 tiny skeletons were discovered. It seems that it was in fact used as a form of birth control for those who could not afford the extra mouth to feed or perhaps because of deformity. The most famous case of the Roman practice of exposure of infants lies in its history, in the case of the previously mentioned Romulus and Remus who were left outside to die by their wicked uncle and, as legend has it, were discovered by a she wolf that took care of them.

When Emperor Constantine (AD 285–337) came to power he legalised the sale of unwanted infants, which sounds truly appalling to our modern sensibilities, but it was at least one step up from exposure! Fortunately exposure did not always occur; the discovery of the twins with syphilis with—we presume—their parents who would have required constant round-the-clock care, proves that there were times when the opposite was true.

Women looked after the running of the house and supervised the day to day practicalities of life, made easier if they could afford slaves. Only rich male children were educated, usually by slaves. Girls were often married off at the tender age of 14, but with childbirth being extremely dangerous many did not live beyond the age of 30.

Herculaneum

Herculaneum, which lies 12 miles to the west of Pompeii, was a small seaside resort enjoyed by wealthy Romans. Although its exact size is as yet still unknown it is thought it would have been between one third and one half the size of Pompeii, with a population of about 5,000. It would have had all the same facilities that Pompeii had to offer but on a more upmarket (albeit smaller) scale. So far excavations have revealed that they had only one theatre, a palestra and two baths, the forum baths and the suburban baths, but it was enough to meet the needs of the smaller population.

Herculaneum, like Pompeii was a walled city, having also participated in the Italic wars, and just like Pompeii was also fed water

8 College of the Augustales at Herculaneum.

by the same aqueduct. Rich with sea view villas, and a pedestrianized main thoroughfare, known as the Decmanus Maximus, it too had its shops and temples. It even had a College of the Augustales, a cult where freedmen, or ex-slaves, who were banned from holding priestly positions in other temples, could train to be priests in the cult of Emperor worship.

One of the ways in which Herculaneum differed from Pompeii was in its streets. Called cardines, there have been five uncovered to date and these run downhill from north to south. Because of this natural drainage there are no pedestrian stepping stones. All these 'modern' conveniences helped to make life good in Pompeii and Herculaneum, but things were about to take an ominous turn.

Notes

1 **Bulwer-Lytton, Baron, Edward George,** *Days of Pompeii* (Kindle edition e-book)

2 **Wallace-Hadrill, Andrew,** *Houses and Society in Pompeii and Herculaneum* (Chichester, West Sussex: Princeton University Press, 1994), p. 12

3 http://www.guardian.co.uk/science/2011/sep/22/pompeii-red-yellow

4 **Beard, Mary,** *Pompeii: The Life of a Roman Town* (London: Profile Books Ltd, 2010), p. 205

5 **Cooley, Alison** and **Cooley, M.G.L.,** *Pompeii: a sourcebook* (London: Routledge, 2004), p. 61.

6 **Wilkinson, Paul,** *Pompeii: The Last Day* (London: BBC Book, BBC Worldwide Ltd, 2003), p. 134.

7 **Pliny the Younger,** http://www.earlychristianwritings.com/pliny.html—see section marked 'Pliny the Younger on Christians'.

8 Ibid.

9 **Beard, Mary,** *Pompeii: The Life of a Roman Town*, p. 80.

10 http://www.bbc.co.uk/news/world-europe-11952322.

The trembling earth

God is our refuge and strength, an ever-present help in trouble. Therefore we will not fear, though the earth give way and the mountains fall into the heart of the sea, though its waters roar and foam and the mountains quake with their surging.   Psalm 46:1–3

T he people of Campania were used to the ground moving beneath their feet, having felt the trembling of the earth many times. Sometimes, if the earth shook very hard, things would get broken but they just accepted it as part of their life. On 5 February AD 62 around midday the people of Campania were rocked by an earthquake

9   The crumbling walls of Pompeii and the ever dominant Vesuvius in the background.

whose epicentre was Pompeii, but this time it was different—this time it was 'the big one', measuring approximately (so experts surmise) anywhere between 5 and 7 on the Richter Scale.

According to the historian Seneca 'it inflicted great destruction on Campania, a region which has never been safe from this evil, yet which has remained undamaged and has often got off with a fright. For part of the town of Herculaneum too fell down and even the structures that remain are unstable, and the colony of Nuceria, though it escaped disaster, nevertheless is not without complaint. Naples too lost many private buildings, but no public ones, being stricken only lightly by the great disaster; even villas have collapsed, everywhere things shook without damage.'[1]

In Pompeii, the centre of the earthquake zone, buildings swayed and collapsed and the main reservoir for the aqueduct was damaged, affecting the fresh water supply to the city. There is even a report of how a giant chasm opened up in the countryside swallowing a flock of about six hundred sheep. People were left bruised and shocked but, strangely, only one fatality was recorded, that of Vestal Virgin Laelia. As seismologists often say: 'Earthquakes don't kill people, buildings do'.

Time to leave?

The psychological impact of the earthquake was far greater than the visual and physical damage it caused. Seneca sums it up very well when he says 'we must seek solace for the anxious and dispel overmastering fear. For what can any one believe quite safe if the world itself is shaken, and its most solid parts totter to their fall? Where, indeed, can our fears have limit if the one thing immovably fixed, which upholds all other things in dependence on it, begins to rock, and the earth lose its chief characteristic, stability? What refuge can our weak bodies find? Whither shall anxious ones flee when fear springs from the ground and is drawn up from earth's foundations? If roofs at any time begin to crack and premonitions of fall are given, there is general panic: all hurry pell-mell out of doors, they abandon their household treasures, and trust for safety to the public street. But if the earth itself stir up destruction, what refuge or help can we look for? If this solid globe, which upholds and defends us, upon which our cities are built, which has been called by some the world's foundation, stagger and remove, wither are we to turn?'²

Many of the population no longer felt safe in their own homes. It was reported that strong aftershocks and tremors were felt for at least seven days after the initial earthquake. No relief funds were forthcoming from Emperor Nero, due it was thought to the earlier mentioned incident in the amphitheatre. Some houses and civic buildings were now uninhabitable. Many people, seeing the whole incident as an act of divine displeasure, left never to return. However, a few would stay and try to

10 House of the Vetti; a household shrine (lararium) with its guardian or gods (lares) who were thought to protect the family from external threats. The snake was also looked upon as a guardian spirit.

rebuild, offering more sacrifices to their gods in the vain hope that they would keep them safe. But their gods weren't listening!

Notes

1   Cooley, **Alison E.** and **Cooley, M.G.L.,** *Pompeii: A Source Book* (London: Routledge, 2004), p. 29

2   **Seneca,** *Naturales Queaestiones* Book VI (http://naturalesquaestiones.blogspot.co.uk/2009/08/book-vi-tr-john-clarke.html) sections 222 Physical Science Bk, vi 4 & 5.

Eruption

The heavens will disappear with a roar; the elements will be destroyed by fire, and the earth and everything in it will be laid bare.   2 Peter 3:10

Fields of fire

A study of the region of Campania and the bay of Naples makes it evident that the inhabitants would have been very conscious of volcanic activity. Italy has the only active volcanoes in mainland Europe, this being due to the country's close proximity to both the Eurasian and African tectonic plates, which causes constant trouble from volcanoes and earthquakes.

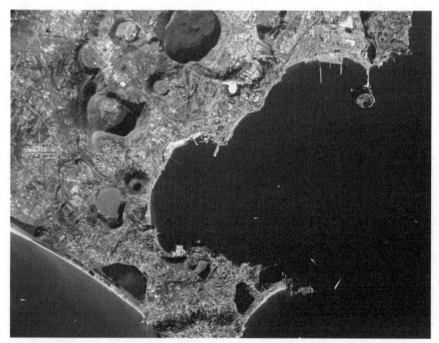

11   Aerial shot of Puzzuoli and the Phlegrean Fields.

Just to the north of Naples are the Phlegrean Fields or 'fields of fire', a 13km-wide barren, lunar-looking landscape with a myriad of mini cones emitting a mist or haze of dangerous gasses (sulphur, carbon dioxide and arsenic) which hangs above pools of hot mud. With the deformation of the land, subject to rising and falling, there would have been evidence of this activity even in Roman times—as proven by the remains of submerged Roman temples. Even in recent times, residents of Pozzuoli (formerly Puteoli) saw the land rise a staggering 3.5 metres in just a few months.

There are in fact three active volcanoes in Italy and ten dormant. Mount Stromboli, on Stromboli one of the Aeolian Islands north of Sicily; Mount Etna located on the Isle of Sicily itself—two volcanoes which have constantly erupted throughout history; and, of course, Vesuvius.

Strabo, a Greek historian who lived from 64 BC to AD 25, writing long before the eruption of AD 79 states 'Mount Vesuvius is situated above these places and people live all around on very beautiful farms, except at the summit. This is flat for the main part, but completely unfruitful, like ashes to look at and it displays porous hollows of rocks blackened on the surface, as if devoured by fire. As a result, one would deduce that this area was previously on fire and held craters of fire, and that it was extinguished when the fuel failed. Perhaps this is also the reason for the fruitfulness of the surrounding area, just as at Catana they say that the part covered by ash carried up by the fire of Etna made the country suited to vine-growing.'[1]

A sleeping dragon

However, although it is likely they understood what a volcano was, it is also likely that Vesuvius had not erupted in living memory. The soil around the mountain was rich, and crops, particularly grapes, grew plentifully, making Campania a region well known for its wines. It is generally believed that Vesuvius at the time of the AD 79 eruption was covered in grass and trees possibly all the way to the summit. The earth continued to tremble every so often but 18 years had now passed since the big earthquake and things had definitely quietened down. Life continued as normal and, although the population had dwindled it had been boosted by a necessary influx of builders, carpenters, labourers and other tradespeople in an effort to restore the city to its former glory.

The now late Emperor Vespasian had sent money to fund a rebuilding scheme, together with one of his magistrates, Suedius Clemens, to restore order. There appeared to have been some sort of social unrest and a problem with squatters. It would seem that a few people had taken advantage of Pompeii's unfortunate situation by taking up residence on public property. Once the land had been reclaimed and order restored, rebuilding work began. Nonetheless the earthquake was a warning and an indication of the horror that was to come.

24 August AD 79[3]

As was normal for that time of year, the morning brought beautiful, hot, sunny weather. It was to be a time of rejoicing. Sixty years earlier the Emperor Augustus had died and been deified. The citizens of Pompeii had been celebrating for some days and they were now preparing to celebrate the Vulcanalia, a time of worship to the god Vulcan (god of the forge and metal working and, ironically, god of destructive fire!). In order that he would prevent the crops being consumed by the hot summer sun they would shower Vulcan with gifts. There would be large bonfires and sacrifices of live fish and small animals, which would act as stand-ins for the people themselves. The only fly in the ointment, so to speak, was that the people had noticed the earth tremors were becoming more frequent again.

An ordinary day

The hustle and bustle of the early morning had already begun with shopkeepers opening up in preparation for the day of celebration. Market traders, who had lined the entrance roads into Pompeii with booths, were also setting up shop. The baker had risen early; he kneaded the dough and rolled it into circular loaves, cutting into the top an asterisk which would allow the dough to open during cooking and finally placing it inside the oven. Behind him, tethered to the large millstone, was a blindfolded mule; it certainly was not a day of celebration for the poor animal. The meat sellers were preparing fish, stripping them of their scales and the thermopolium – fast food –vendors were ensuring that their terracotta vessels were full of meat stew and wine ready for their customers. Just like the fish and chip shops of today they even had a form of ketchup, not made of tomatoes but a salted rotting fish sauce which the population seemed to enjoy with everything.

Three painters turned up at a house in the Via dell' Abbondanza to finish the redecorating work they had begun; if they could get the job done in time maybe they too could join in the celebration. Slaves too would have to rise early and make the preparations necessary for their owners to enjoy the day.

But inside Vesuvius all was not quiet. Magma, which is called lava only when it flows outside of the volcano, was forcing its way up through the earth's crust into the cracks within the volcano causing the rock to split and the earth to shudder. It is very probable that the caldera, or crater, at the top was sealed by a crust of earth and solidified lava, causing an increase in the build-up of gasses and magma rather like a cork in a bottle of fizzy lemonade that's been shaken. Vesuvius was to all intents and purposes like a giant pressure cooker.

The beginning of the end

Sometime in the early morning, the people of Pompeii felt the earth jolt violently beneath their feet, sending them reeling while at the same time a sonic boom rattled window shutters and doors, as well as eardrums, as

Vesuvius exploded into life with a deafening roar. A thick black cloud of ash and pumice began to thrust skywards from the top of the mountain as the thin crust at the top of the volcano finally gave way. Forming the now familiar umbrella shape, the thick billowing smoke began to darken the sky as the cloud column soared more than two miles into the atmosphere. The citizens of Pompeii, rudely awakened, would no doubt have rushed to their windows and doors in time to see the sky beginning to blacken as ash and pumice, blown by the wind, began to rain down upon the people.

The eruption began its work in earnest. Every second a staggering 10,000 tonnes of debris was ejected from the volcano, reaching speeds in excess of 500 miles per hour. The size of the 'pumice' ranged anywhere between half an inch (1.3cm) and six inches (15cm) across, occasionally the larger ones causing damage to windows, doors and people. The sea shore soon became choked as the sea currents pushed the floating pumice towards the beach, making it impossible to launch any vessels as a means of escape for the populace from the terror that was upon them. Panic and fear would have gripped the people as Vesuvius revealed itself to be very much alive. Some decided that now was the time to run and began to flee to the countryside while others stayed, some because they had no choice through infirmity or sickness, others because they wanted to see if it would all just fizzle out and still others because they were no doubt too terrified even to run. The air would have become thick and heavy with a deadly cocktail of noxious gases: carbon dioxide, hydrogen, carbon monoxide and sulphur dioxide. The people who stayed would no doubt have prayed to their gods hoping that they would protect them.

Types of volcano

There are two main types of volcano: shield and composite. Shield volcanoes build, as in Hawaii where whole islands have been created out of the sea. Composite volcanoes destroy, as in cases such as Mount St Helen's or Krakatoa. Eruptions are measured on a VEI or Volcanic

Explosivity Index from 0 to 8, zero being non-explosive and eight being super volcano—all singing all dancing end of the world type, as it is expected that the one in Yellowstone National Park will be, when and if it explodes. Points are given for the volume of products ejected from a volcano, the eruption cloud height and based on observations, i.e. gentle, mega or colossal. For instance, Krakatoa (1883) was believed to have been a 6, Mount St Helens (1980) was a 5, Tambora (1815) was, it is thought, a 7. There has not been a VEI 8 in living memory. Vesuvius in AD 79 is believed to have been a 5.

Through someone else's eyes

A lot of what we know about the Vesuvius eruption that destroyed Pompeii is based on an eyewitness account written down by the bureaucrat Pliny the Younger. Then a youth of 18, he was on a long-term visit with his uncle Pliny the Elder, who lived around the north-west tip of

12 Map showing the fallout from the AD 79 eruption.

the bay of Naples at the imperial naval base of Misenum, some 19 miles/13.57km from Vesuvius. As well as being Naval Commander, Pliny the Elder was noted for being an encyclopaedist; his 37-volume *Naturalis Historia* (Natural History) was famous even in Roman times. At about lunchtime, Pliny the Elder had finished taking his bath, of which he had a private set, and had settled down to work on his book. Pliny the Younger's mother wandered out on to the terrace to look across the bay and was perplexed by a strange cloud in the distance, which she reported looked like a large umbrella pine tree. She called out to both men who joined her on the terrace where they gazed upon the phenomenon and, being the true scientist, Pliny the Elder determined to go and get a closer look.

A rescue attempt

Before he could give orders for a boat to be made ready, a message arrived from Rectina, wife of his old friend Tascius, saying she was trapped in her house at the foot of the mountain and that escape was impossible except by sea and please could he come to help her. (How the message was delivered is not stated in Pliny's account though it seems likely that it was carried by a slave who, if he had been hit by the falling pumice, would not have mattered! Historians also speculate that the eruption must have begun in the early morning in order for the cloud column to be visible and to allow time for the messenger to reach Misenum).

As Pliny himself says of his uncle 'he changed his plans and what he had begun in a spirit of enquiry, he completed as a hero. He ordered warships to be launched and embarked, aiming to bring help to many others beside Rectina (for the beautiful coastline was thickly populated). He hurried to the place from which others were fleeing and steered his course straight for danger. So fearless was he that he dictated notes on each movement and change in shape of the disaster as he observed them.'[2]

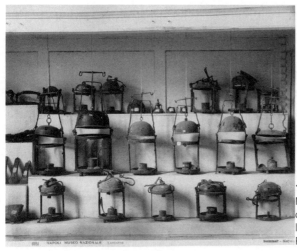

13 Display in Naples Museum; a large number of clay oil lamps and bronze lanterns were recovered from Pompeii.

The people of Herculaneum had so far been untouched by what was happening. Although they were now directly under the umbrella-like cloud, the wind was blowing towards Pompeii and away from the city, and would have spared them much of the pelting pumice. They would obviously have felt the constant earth tremors and heard the roar of the mountain but at the moment they were merely spectators with a ring side seat—but for them the clock was ticking.

Flee while you can

A few hours after the eruption the sky over Pompeii was completely dark, the summer sun obliterated by the thick cloud. The people lit candles and oil lamps and huddled indoors, afraid to venture out. Though it was evident that the need for evacuation was imminent and some did leave, many stayed possibly afraid of the roar of the mountain and the constant bombardment from above. Visibility would have been practically zero and in the darkened streets disorientation would have caused panic and mayhem. The pumice would have felt like acid rain, stinging the eyes and bruising the skin, while the thick black acrid air would have made breathing difficult. Staying indoors would have seemed a much safer option.

Meanwhile the pumice on the roofs was getting heavier and in many places was now over fifteen inches (37cm) thick and the weight upon the tiles, together with the constant shaking of the foundations by the on-going earth tremors, was beginning to cause the roofs and buildings to collapse, crushing those inside. Some people now had no choice but to venture outside in a bid to find stronger shelter, making head coverings of some kind in an effort to afford themselves some protection while they tried to make a run for it. They would have found walking heavy going, as they had to wade through more than 100 million tonnes of pumice which in places was up to 20 inches (50cm) thick and struggling to breathe in the dense air.

Looking up through the great black cloud which hung over the city they would have been able to see lightning flashes, as the billowing smoke reached a height of nine to ten miles. Pliny the Elder found himself blocked in his rescue mission by the charred and blackened pumice which littered the sea. Unable to land at Pompeii he headed for Stabiae, where another friend, Pomponianus lived.

Putting on a brave face

Pliny the Younger writes 'he embraced, consoled and encouraged the fearful Pomponianus, and in order to lessen his friend's fear by his own assurance, he ordered that he be taken to the baths.'[4] Pliny the Elder is believed to have been rather corpulent in size, with breathing difficulties possibly due to asthma or bronchitis, so it is very probable that he was carried by slaves to the baths.

At about 7.00 p.m. the citizens of Herculaneum watched with a morbid curiosity as the cloud column continued to rise, now 16 miles (26km) above the crater of Vesuvius. (To put this into perspective this is the second layer of earth's atmosphere: the stratosphere. It is here that the ozone layer can be found; commercial aeroplanes cannot fly this high.) They could see flashes of lightning and occasionally explosions of red-hot lava spurting from the crater. Buildings were beginning to collapse through the constant and violent earth tremors. Many had already deserted the town, but some took shelter on the beach in the vaults or boat huts believing no doubt that the worst would pass them by and they just had to wait it out.

Pliny the Elder, having had his bath, sat down and dined with his friend, making light and cheerful conversation, declaring the flashes of lava and lightning to be 'fires abandoned by country folk in their panic and villas that were burning through being left uninhabited.'[5] After dining he retired to bed.

Notes

1 **Cooley, Alison E.** and **Cooley, M.G.L.,** *Pompeii: A Source Book* (London: Routledge, 2004), p. 32.

2 Ibid. p. 33.

3 The month of October has also been suggested based on several factors one being a bag of coins found with a female victim. But for the purposes of this account I have gone with the traditional date.

4 Ibid. p. 33.

5 Ibid. pp. 33–34.

The end is nigh!

The sun and sky were darkened by the smoke from the Abyss.   Revelation 9:2

25 August AD 79

In the early hours of the morning things took a dramatic turn for the worse. Herculaneum and Oplontis, which up until that point had still been untouched by the eruption, were about to experience the full force of Mount Vesuvius' fury. The material in the cloud column was now so dense that it could no longer be supported and the column collapsed back down the sides of the volcano, producing a deadly pyroclastic flow.

The term pyroclastic is made up of two Greek words pyro (fire) and klastos (broken) and describes the materials formed by the breaking up of magma and rock during an eruption. There is ash made up of pyroclastic

14 Eruption of Mount Mayon in the Philippines, showing the sheer power and horror of pyroclastic flow.

material of finely ground rock and magma, but there are also lapilli, blocks or bombs, which are made up of larger, denser, pyroclastic material.

An avalanche of pulverised debris hurtled down the mountain at speeds of anywhere up to 600 miles per hour, but being pushed ahead of it was a super-heated deadly gas cloud. There was nowhere to go, no way to outrun this tidal wave of destruction as it blasted through Herculaneum and Oplontis, leaving buildings intact but killing all in its path. It sped through streets and into houses and shops, hurtling its way through every part of the city. This silent killer would have enveloped the now sleepy people of Herculaneum who had camped all night on the beach or had stayed in the nearby brick boat huts, waiting for it all to fizzle out. In Oplontis many cowered in the seemingly solid basement of a large warehouse, no doubt thinking they would be safe there, but they too would have succumbed to the deadly cloud.

Death comes swiftly

Within the gas cloud temperatures would probably have exceeded a staggering 400°C/750°F, and death would have been mercifully quick. Burning hot steam, gas, particles of dust and pumice would be breathed in through the nose and mouth, searing the windpipe and lungs and causing almost instantaneous asphyxiation. Brains would boil within the skull, bones shatter and teeth disintegrate as people were flash-boiled alive.

Just seconds later Herculaneum was hit by the second wave, heavier and denser than the gas surge, this would have contained volcanic material as well as debris it picked up on its way down the mountainside. Anything in the path of this flow would simply have been buried, but the people of Herculaneum would have known nothing of this for they would have already perished in the first surge; their flesh, sinews and brains now replaced with solidified ash and debris. Similarly, when a second pyroclastic surge hit the town at around 2.00 a.m. there would have been nobody left alive to notice or care.

Chapter 5

The end for Pliny

At around 6.00 a.m., at Stabiae, Pliny the Elder had to be woken up. Pliny the Younger now takes up the story as he writes:

'But the level of the courtyard from which his rooms were approached had so risen, by being filled with ashes mixed with pumice, that any further delay in the bedroom would have prevented escape. On being woken, he went out and returned to Pomponianus and the others who had remained awake. They consulted together whether to stay indoors or wander in the open. For the buildings were shaking with frequent and severe tremors and seemed to be swaying to and fro as if removed from their own foundations. Then again, in the open air there was the fear of falling pumice stones, even though these were light and porous. On comparing the dangers, they chose the latter (in my uncle's case reason won out; but fear in the case of the others). They put cushions on their heads, tied with cloth, as protection against falling objects. Now it was day elsewhere; there it was night, blacker and denser than any night, though many torches and various lights broke it up.'[1]

It appears that Pliny the Elder, Pomponianus and his household tried yet again to go down to the boats and see if they could launch, but finding the sea 'high, and hostile',[2] Pliny the Elder lay down on a tarpaulin. Being overweight and already suffering with breathing difficulties, combined with the heavy amounts of sulphur and carbon dioxide in the air, he would have found breathing extremely painful. It is thought that about this time a huge pyroclastic surge hit Oplontis and fanned out to encompass Pompeii, the edge of which could have reached the party on the beach. As the rest of the group began to travel on without him, Pliny the Elder attempted to raise himself with the assistance of his slaves but was overcome probably by the thick noxious gases and fell back down dead. His body would later be recovered by Pliny the Younger 'intact, uninjured, covered and just as he had been dressed: the appearance of the body was more like someone asleep than dead.'[3]

The final death knell

Seconds before, Pompeii itself had succumbed to this same pyroclastic surge. Many of those that remained had had no choice but to leave their homes as the buildings, like those at Stabiae, were shaking and beginning to collapse under the sheer weight of ash and pumice. As the mountain's column of ash and debris collapsed again, this pyroclastic surge now headed straight for Pompeii.

Inside the house of Julius Polybius, the freedman, he and his family huddled together. The decorators that had been next door had fled many hours ago leaving their paint cans and brushes where they had dropped them. But for Polybius' household they had no choice, they had to stay. The ten family members and two slaves had already moved to the back of the house, the front having collapsed under the sheer weight of the mounting pumice. They couldn't leave, for one of his daughters was heavily pregnant and her time was very near; they would just 'ride the storm'.

Fearing the worst, many of the citizens of Pompeii were only now beginning to leave, braving the darkness and the onslaught of stones and pumice, but they had left it too late. As they watched in horror the fast approaching wall of blackness raced down Vesuvius towards them. A tethered dog arched his back and tried desperately to bite through his leash in an effort to free himself, a man wrapped his tunic around his mouth in order to avoid the choking acrid air. A mother clung to her child, shielding it with her body in an effort to protect it, a husband embraced his wife hiding her face in his chest. One family hitched up their tunics and ran, taking what valuables they could carry with them but making it only as far as the necropolis (the local cemetery). A priest cradled the temple treasure he had wrapped in a linen cloth, a woman clutched at her silver lucky charm and a young man his dagger. A male slave desperately tried to run from the oncoming wave, his efforts hampered by the iron shackles around his ankles. Rich, poor, young, old, slave and free all were caught, trapped by the fast-flowing deadly cloud.

Among those who had left it too late to leave were Princess Drusilla and her son, Marcus Antonius Agrippa. Drusilla was married to Felix, Procurator of Judea. She had listened to the apostle Paul when he had preached the gospel to both Agrippa and her sister Bernice, before he had finally been shipped off to Rome. One can only speculate what went through her mind during those last few minutes, but now she would find out what it was like to stand before the King of Glory and face his eternal judgement.

A painful end

In his book *Pompeii: The Last Day*, Paul Wilkinson writes 'hot ash blasted in through chinks in doors and windows, holes in roofs. It killed most of the remaining inhabitants of Pompeii, but death was not instantaneous. With the first breath, hot gas and ash were inhaled, causing the lungs to fill with fluid: it was like swallowing fire. The second breath took in more ash, which mixed with the fluid to create a wet cement in the lungs and windpipe. The third inhalation thickened the cement, causing the victims to gasp for breath—and suffocate because death was slightly slower than in the Herculaneum boatsheds, people writhed in agony on the ground, unable to breathe, which accounts for the contorted positions of some of the bodies.'4 Mercifully we are talking about seconds and not minutes.

It's time to go

In Misenum, Pliny the Younger and his mother had watched the spectacle with growing horror. He writes 'For many days previously there had been earth tremors, less alarming because frequent in Campania; but that night they grew so strong that it seemed everything was not so much being moved, but being overturned. My mother burst into my bedroom: I was getting up anyway but would have been woken had I been asleep. We sat in the courtyard of the house, which formed a small area separating

15 Caught in a moment; a victim's final struggles are captured forever.

the sea from the living quarters. I am not sure whether I should call it brave or foolish (I was seventeen at the time) but I called for a book of Livy and as if reading for pleasure I continued to make the summaries I had begun. Then a friend of my uncle, who had recently come to visit him from Spain, saw my mother and me sitting down, and me actually reading, and attacked her over-indulgence and my complacency. I remained as eagerly engrossed in my book.

'Now it was the first hour of daylight, but the light was still weak and uncertain. Now the surrounding buildings were shaking and although we were in the open, being in a confined space, we were in great and real danger from the house collapsing. Then finally we decided to leave the town: a dazed mob followed us, preferring someone else's plan to their own—the nearest they could get to prudence in their panic. They hurried us on our way, pressing in a thick crowd behind us. Once out of the built-up area we stopped. There we experienced many remarkable and terrifying phenomena. The carriages which we had ordered to be brought began to move in different directions although the ground was quite level and they did not even stay still when secured by stones placed in their tracks. In addition we watched the sea apparently sucked out and driven back by the earthquake. Certainly the shoreline had advanced and stranded many sea creatures on dry sand. On the other side, a terrifying black cloud, split by twisted blasts of fire shooting in different directions, gaped to reveal long fiery shapes, similar to flashes of lightning only bigger.'[5]

An enveloping darkness

Many scholars feel that what Pliny the Younger is describing with the withdrawal of the sea is a tsunami associated with the climax of a later eruption. As Pliny and his mother fled Misenum, which was at least 18 miles from the eruption, the final pyroclastic surge swept down the slopes of Mount Vesuvius. Such a truly enormous surge would have finished off what the others had begun. It swept through Pompeii at a tremendous speed, killing anyone left alive and swept on and out in all directions seeking out those who had evacuated to the country and annihilating hundreds. Crossing the sea, the pyroclastic surge began to lose its momentum, but it reached Misenum and engulfed those that were fleeing to the countryside.

Once again Pliny the Younger paints a dramatic picture as he writes 'Now ash was falling, though still lightly. I looked back: behind our backs loomed thick blackness, which like a torrent pursued us, spreading over the earth. "Let us turn aside," I said, "while we can see, to avoid being knocked down and trampled on in the darkness by the crowd around us." We had only just sat down when darkness fell, not like a moonless or cloudy night, but like when a light is extinguished in a closed room. You could hear women screaming, babies wailing, men shouting: some were calling out for their parents, others for their children, others

16 The death of Pliny the Elder, while he lies dying on the tarpaulin in the background the rest of the party is depicted fleeing the scene. Printed in the French newspaper *Le Monde Illustré* in 1888.

for their spouses, and trying to recognise their voices; some lamented their own misfortune, others that of their relatives; there was some who in their fear of dying prayed for death; many raised their hands to the gods; more still concluded that there were no gods and that this was the world's final and everlasting night.'[6]

Aftermath

After two days, and at least six pyroclastic surges and flows, the city of Herculaneum had disappeared beneath 75 feet (23 metres) of volcanic material. Pompeii too was buried although not as deeply, the second storeys of some of the taller buildings could still be seen above 10 feet (3 metres) of ash. The coastline in the bay of Naples had changed forever, with the sea receding 1.5km (just under a mile).

Emperor Titus declared a state of emergency and, in a similar way to the political leaders of today, visited the disaster area himself. He appointed two ex-consuls to oversee the distribution of relief funds, into which he personally had donated monies, to those survivors who had lost all in the catastrophe. There were many refugees who fled to other parts of Campania; a section of Naples was named after survivors who settled there.

At Herculaneum all attempts at exhumation were abandoned; they simply could find no trace of the town. At Pompeii, however, it was possible to identify landmarks and streets because of the structures which stood above the ash settlement and there is clear evidence of salvaging and plundering taking place in the ruins of the city. Many buildings are riddled with holes which were dug not to recover people but marble, items of value, precious metals and even statues. Eventually, when they believed they had gathered all they could, the stones themselves were used to re-build houses and other structures. Grass grew over the top and the remains of Pompeii disappeared from view.

For a brief moment in history time seemed to stop and people sat up and took note, thought about death and eternity but then, as so often is the case, time moved on and the people would have put such thoughts out of their minds.

Notes

1 **Cooley, Alison E.** and **Cooley, M.G.L.,** *Pompeii: A Source Book* (London: Routledge, 2004), p. 34

2 Ibid.

3 Ibid.

4 **Wilkinson, Paul,** *Pompeii: The Last Day* (London: BBC Books, 2003), p. 67

5 **Cooley, Alison E.** and **Cooley, M.G.L.,** p. 36

6 Ibid. p. 37

Accidental Discovery

Beneath, o'ergrown with grass, or wreathed with flowers,
Lie tombs and temples, columns, baths and towers.
As if, in mockery, Nature seems to dress
In all her charms the beauteous wilderness,
And bids her gayest flowerets twine and bloom
In sweet profusion o'er a city's tomb.

Pompeii by Thomas Babbington Macaulay[1]

By the Middle Ages Pompeii and Herculaneum had become almost mythical in their status: people knew that once there had been a great city known locally as 'la Civita', but no one knew where it was or that their homes and farms were built on top of the ruins. Occasionally some artefact would be dug up during ploughing but no real relevance was given to it.

Roger Ling, in his book *Pompeii: History, Life and Afterlife*, says 'In 1689 an excavation in search of water yielded further inscriptions, one of which apparently included a specific reference to Pompeii. A contemporary historian correctly divined that Civita was the site of Pompeii and, though others were sceptical, the same view was taken by Giuseppe Macrini, who in 1693 reported having himself seen well preserved remains of buried buildings.'[2]

But it was not until 1709 that a major discovery was made, and that was not at Pompeii but Herculaneum.

A decorating spree

On 7 July 1707 Austria took over Naples from the Spanish; it was just one link in a long line of successive foreign victories by various nations seeking to rule Italy. One particular Austrian general, Prince d'Elboeuf, had decided to build himself a villa in the region. In 1709 news reached him of a remarkable discovery made by a farmer who, in the course of digging a well, tunnelled down and found, not water, but an underground building with amazing wall paintings (this would later be identified as the theatre). Wasting no time, Prince d'Elboeuf bought the land from the farmer, widened the well, made several more tunnels down into the area and decorated his new villa with the marble statues and sculptures which he found there.

Later the land came once again into the hands of the Spanish who continued the excavation of the well. It was, therefore, Spanish engineer Rocque Joachin de Alcubierre who discovered that the site was in fact a theatre and a part of the long lost Herculaneum. The work was hard going, the volcanic material being densely packed and deep, but still the discoveries kept coming.

Unfortunately in those early days of archaeology the technology to preserve the artefacts did not exist at this time and many wonderful items were lost never to be seen again. There were also incredible acts of what

17 Excavation and reconstruction of the House of Vetti during the nineteenth century.

can only be described as wanton destruction. In *Pompeii and Herculaneum (Digging Up the Past)*, author Peter Hicks states 'under Alcubierre pieces of a racing chariot and some bronze horses were discovered. A sculptor named Joseph Canart was bought in to restore them, but having inspected them he decided they were beyond repair. Instead of restoring them he melted down the body of the charioteer and cast it into medals, figurines of saints and ornaments.[3]

Perhaps the most amazing of these finds was what is now called the Villa of the Papyri, believed to have been the seaside retreat of Julius Caesar's father-in-law, so called because a whole library of tightly rolled scrolls were unearthed on the site. Over one thousand burnt papyri were found loaded into cases, presumably with the intention that they be evacuated. Many were destroyed in failed attempts to unroll these carbonised scrolls, crumbling into dust their contents lost forever, until finally it was decided to store them until the technology existed that could read them safely. It is only in recent years that efforts have been made again to unravel their secrets; using x-rays and digital imaging scientists are now, finally, beginning to read the scrolls.

What's in a name

All the names given to the streets, buildings and gates are modern, given by the person who made the discovery, and are usually based either on an artefact recovered from the site or on the name of the person whom they believed lived there. For example at Herculaneum we have the House of the Wooden Partition, named after a beautifully preserved wooden partition found there, or the House of the Beautiful Courtyard named for obvious reasons. At Pompeii there is the House of the Surgeon named after the surgical implements discovered, the House of Venus in the Sea Shell after a mural on the wall, or the House of the Faun named for the bronze statue of a Faun discovered on the site.

18 Replica of the faun discovered at the 'House of the Faun' wrongly placed upon a pedestal within the impluvium.

Images of the dead

In the early days of excavation artefacts were just dug up merely for their monetary value and removed to another location where they could be put on display or sold. No thought was given to logging where they had been found or keeping them in situ to preserve a sense of wholeness to the scene, or to their historical value. It wasn't until Giuseppe Fiorelli became inspector of the excavations in 1860 that the archaeology became more systematic. It was Fiorelli who numbered every building then discovered on the site, giving each one three numbers; region, insula (block of houses or individual house) and doorway. This system is still used today. He also instigated the practice of excavating from the top downwards, instead of from street level up, and it was also Fiorelli who noted the strange 'cavities' which so often appeared during excavations and realised they were in fact indentations left by the people and animals who died in the AD 79 eruption, their bodies having rotted away. Using a special technique of pouring plaster into the holes he managed to preserve for us today a way to see the last death throes of the poor inhabitants that perished.

In 1867 W.D. Howells, American literary critic and short story writer, was obviously struck by the revealed remains and wrote 'The man in the last struggle has thrown himself upon his back and taken in his doom sturdily—there is a sublime calm in his rigid figure. The women lie upon their faces, their limbs tossed and distorted, their drapery tangled and heaped about them, and in every fibre you see how hard they died. One presses her face into her handkerchief to draw one last breath unmixed with scalding steam; another's arms are wildly thrown abroad to clutch at help; another's hand is appealingly raised, and on her slight fingers you see the silver hoops with which her poor dead vanity adorned them.'[4]

Fiorelli put the death toll in Pompeii at about 2,000, a figure which is thought by many to be fairly accurate. So far, 1,150 'bodies' have been recovered, the majority of which were found above the initial pumice fall. However this figure does not allow for the fact that in the early days of the city's discovery no one was interested in the 'cavities' or human remains and many were destroyed. Neither have excavations extended much beyond the walls of Pompeii; it is only recently that historians have begun to look beyond these walls.

At Herculaneum for a long time very few bodies were recovered, leading to the belief that many had fled and survived. It was not until 1981 that Dr Giuseppe Maggi began to find the remains of the victims sheltering in the boat houses and on the beaches—300 to date.

Who's who

Even in the nineteenth century, Pompeii and Herculaneum had become well-known tourist attractions. When the Crystal Palace Exhibition was relocated in 1854 from Hyde Park to Sydenham, it had as one of its 'courts' a replica of a grand Pompeian house.

Pompeii became popular with the rich and famous. In *Pictures from Italy*, Charles Dickens wrote 'see, at every turn, the familiar tokens of human habitation and everyday pursuits; the chafing of the bucket-rope in the stone rim of the exhausted well; the track of carriage wheels in the pavement of the street; the marks of drinking vessels on the stone counter of the wine shop; the amphorae in private cellars, stored away so many hundred years ago, and undisturbed to this hour—all rendering the solitude and deadly lonesomeness of the place ten thousand times more solemn than if the volcano, in its fury, had swept the city from the earth, and sunk it in the bottom of the sea.'[5]

American author Mark Twain visited the site during his trip to Europe, and although not taken with the Neapolitans, was clearly impressed with Pompeii. He wrote 'They pronounce it "Pom-pay-e". I always had an idea that you went down into Pompeii with torches, by the way of damp, dark stairways, just as you do in silver mines, and traversed gloomy tunnels with lava overhead and something on either hand like

19 Giuseppe Fiorelli, director of excavations (1860–75).

dilapidated prisons gouged out of the solid earth, that faintly resembled houses. But you do nothing of the kind. Fully one half of the buried city, perhaps, is completely exhumed and thrown open freely to the light of day.'6

Frozen in time

The two cities were like perfectly preserved time capsules and therefore ideal for historical study. Until their discovery everything historians knew about the Roman way of life was based on ruins and writings, but here were two cities caught in a moment. At Pompeii they found bread still in the bakery's ovens, dinner on tables, pots and pans still in their cupboards, tableware and jewellery. Houses complete with mosaic floors like the entrance way to the House of the Tragic Poet on which is depicted a rather vicious looking dog on a lead, underneath which are the words 'cave canem' or 'beware of the dog'! Villas like the House of the Vetti with almost wall-to-wall murals, not unlike wallpaper, which when first uncovered still looked colourful, vivid and bright.

Surprisingly, perhaps, a lot of the buildings we see today have been 'reconstructed'. As classicist Mary Beard writes, 'most visitors have no clue that considerable parts of the Large Theatre, for example, and of the forum, as well as some of the most celebrated houses, were almost entirely rebuilt after the war, or that the on-site restaurant was planted on one area of particularly devastating bomb damage.'7

There is also an inordinate amount of ancient graffiti on the walls of Pompeii, which in so many ways reads like graffiti of today; 'Rufus loves Cornelia', 'A small problem gets larger if you ignore it', names and personal messages or political slogans plus, just like today, an awful lot of rude and crude writing, but it gives us a glimpse into the minds of the citizens themselves.

At Herculaneum there are a number of items of carbonised wooden furniture; tables, couches, stairways, doors. Even the remains of a large wooden boat have been found on what would have once been the seashore. Slightly better preserved than her sister, Pompeii, the architecture being more intact, Herculaneum gives an even greater insight into what life would have been like.

On any trip to or any investigation into Pompeii it is the dead that seem to fascinate us the most. Many of the 'plaster cast' bodies have been moved to the Museum at Naples although a few still remain at Pompeii itself. Some of the bodies have gone on display in other countries, to amaze people from around the world.

But perhaps one of the most staggering things is that there is still so much more to be discovered. Only two thirds of Pompeii have been excavated so far and at Herculaneum approximately half is still to be revealed. Excavations have slowed down in an effort to consolidate and widen the knowledge already gained and await the technology that will enable the preservation of the discoveries for future generations.

Going, going, gone

There is, however, a down side to the discovery. In current times the greatest challenge for archaeologists is preservation; now that the cities have been unearthed they are vulnerable to deterioration by the forces of nature and by human activity. Continued seismic activity shakes the already weakened buildings sometimes leading to collapse.

At Herculaneum over two thirds of the site has been closed to the public for safety reasons, neglect and constant erosion by flooding threatening the possible collapse of many buildings. On 6 November 2010 officials arrived at Pompeii to open the site only to find that the Schola Armaturarum Juventus Pompeiani (gladiatorial training school) had collapsed, neglect being the probable culprit. Constantly being exposed to the elements has seen weathering and erosion not just of the buildings and their beautiful murals, but also of the plaster casts of the victims too. In December 2010, after a wall in the 'House of the Moralist' collapsed, UNESCO decided to send a team of experts to Pompeii to investigate the state of conservation.

Wild animals and birds, such as pigeons, foul the streets and murals, the acid in their droppings causing considerable damage. A large number of wild dogs have caused repeated problems at Pompeii, although these days work is underway to try to tame them, feeding them once a day and in many cases neutering them. Grass, weeds and ivy grow up through the paving slabs causing cracking and damage.

Over 2.5 million tourists visit Pompeii every year but they bring with them all sorts of other problems, either deliberately or inadvertently causing damage, particularly vandalism, littering, modern day graffiti or the taking of mementoes and souvenirs. Mary Beard writes 'In 2003 a couple of newly excavated frescoes were prised off their wall, to be found

20 Herculaneum—better preserved than Pompeii—has many carbonised wooden items such as in the House of the Wooden Partition.

three days later at a nearby builder's yard'[8] (presumably to be sold for profit later).

In April 2011 the main street, Decumanus Maximus (Herculaneum), reopened to the public after 20 years of closure, and on 29 November 2011 UNESCO and Italy finally reached an agreement to co-operate on the restoration of Pompeii, but is it perhaps too little too late? In 2012 the Italian government launched an £86 million project to save the site but within less than two weeks part of the external wall collapsed. While Pompeii was undiscovered it was safe but now revealed it seems its future is uncertain; always hanging over it like some dark shadow there is the threat of yet another eruption which could once again bury all before it.

Notes

1 **Macaulay,   Thomas   Babbington,** 'Pompeii',   1819—quoted   on http://www.poemhunter.com/poem/pompeii

2 **Ling, Roger,** *Pompeii: History, Life and Afterlife* (Gloucestershire: Tempus Publishing, 2005), p. 157.

3 **Hicks, Peter,** *Digging Up The Past: Pompeii and Herculaneum* (Hove: Wayland Publishers Ltd, 1995), p. 21.

4 **Howells,   William   Dean,** *Italian   Journeys,*   1867,   quoted   on http://www.gutenberg.org/cache/epub/14276/pg14276.html (Section VIII, part V, 'A Day in Pompeii').

5 **Dickens, Charles,** *Pictures from Italy* (Fairfield, Iowa: 1st World Library—Literary Society, 2004), p. 185.

6 **Twain, Mark,** *The Innocents Abroad* (Hertfordshire: Wordsworth Editions Limited, 2010), p. 210.

7 **Beard, Mary,** *Pompeii: The Life of a Roman Town* (London: Profile Books Ltd, 2008), p. 19.

8 Ibid.

The Unextinguishable Menace

With a deep groan of anguish the mountain burst asunder, and from its side rolled a great stream of molten lava that slowly spread down the slope, consuming, trees, vineyards and dwellings in its path.   *Aunt Jane's Nieces Abroad* by L. Frank Baum[1]

M ount Vesuvius is a medium sized 'humpback' volcano, the peak (or cone) of which sits within another circular crater (caldera) left by a previous eruption of the mountain known as Mount Somma. Towering above the bay of Naples, it stands, at present, approximately 4,000 feet (1,200 metres) high, with Mount Somma reaching 3,714 feet (1,132 metres). There are now thought to be between two and three million people living in its shadow.

The Avellino

The AD 79 eruption of Vesuvius was by no means the first. In 2006 archaeologists uncovered signs of at least one previous eruption dating back to 1780 BC—the Bronze Age. In a section of solidified ash they discovered thousands of footprints all heading in the same direction— away from Vesuvius. Evidence has emerged of a 'Plinian-type' eruption, with a pumice fallout followed by pyroclastic surges. It has been named The Avellino Eruption after the area of Campania where the evidence was discovered, and shows a cataclysmic event which equals and maybe even surpasses the now famous eruption which covered Pompeii. In the city of Nola, perfectly preserved in the ash and lava, is a Bronze Age settlement which is now revealing new details of how the people of that area used to live. These finds are unique; very little is known of what life

21 'The Avellino Eruption': footprints of those who fled preserved in solidified ash dating back to the Bronze Age.

was like in Pompeii before the AD 79 eruption, as officials are naturally reluctant to let archaeologists dig deeper, wanting to preserve the site as a time capsule.

At Nola archaeologists have so far uncovered very little in the way of human remains, and it was originally thought that the inhabitants had read the signs and had the sense to leave while the going was good. But given the sheer magnitude of the eruption, archaeologists are beginning to speculate that it is unlikely that there were many survivors, the fleeing inhabitants being overwhelmed by pyroclastic flows and surges which travelled unhindered over the landscape. Perhaps even more worrying for future generations is that there seems to be evidence that this Bronze Age eruption not only affected areas to the north of Vesuvius but also to the west, with evidence of surges as far away as Naples.

There have been many other known eruptions which have varied in intensity, most being minor with slow lava flows, but nonetheless causing loss of life and property. After the AD 79 eruption Vesuvius seems to have erupted every 100 years or so until 1 June AD 1139 when, after another explosive eruption lasting eight days, it entered a quiescent period. For nearly 500 years Vesuvius lay dormant, with trees and grass growing right up to and on the summit, so that people once again began to forget how dangerous the mountain really was. However, sometime in the evening of the fifteenth or early morning of the sixteenth of December 1631, following a particularly strong earthquake two days previously, the mountain burst into life again, killing 4,000 people living in the vicinity. Vesuvius then began a pattern of minor eruptions every seven years or so.

'A terrible explosion'

While Fiorelli was chief inspector of the site there was yet another eruption. On 27 October 1822 he wrote in his journal 'The terrible explosion of Vesuvius, of which you know, occurred at the beginning of just last week, and I was obliged to flee from Torre Annunziata on Wednesday morning in the direction of Naples on foot, after having spent Tuesday night amidst terrifying thunderous roaring and frightful showers of stones, ash and pumice; consequently I cannot give you information on the excavations of Pompeii.'[2] There are times when archaeology can be a dangerous job.

As the world progressed in terms of technology and media, Vesuvius continued to rumble; in the twentieth century she has erupted three times. In April 1906 she again attracted the world's attention with an eruption that killed 100 people. Watching was American Frank A Perret who, together with Professor Raffaele Vittorio Matteucci, stayed in the observation station to gather data while sending back constant messages to reassure the people of Naples and help avoid a general panic. Both would survive and Perret's observations and comments would become instrumental in the way modern volcanology is run today. Also a witness to the 1906 eruption were a young L. Frank Baum and his wife. Baum included the event in an early novel entitled *Aunt Jane's Nieces Abroad*. Later, of course, he would go on to write *The Wonderful Wizard of Oz*.

There were two more minor eruptions, one in 1929 and the other during the Second World War on 18 March 1944. Between August and September 1943 Pompeii came under attack not just from Vesuvius but from the allies who, believing that enemy troops were billeted there, dropped more than 160 bombs on the site destroying many buildings so that many of them had to be reconstructed later. Even the Director of Pompeii himself was shot when caught in a crossfire which killed his companion.

World War II

Following Italy's changing of sides during the war, one of the units of allied troops stationed in Italy was the United States Army Air Force 340th Bombardment Squad, which was located at the Pompeii Airfield near Terzigno. Following the eruption on 18 March 1944 it was reported that more aircraft were destroyed by the volcano than by enemy activity, although no lives were reported as lost. The falling hot ash melted glass and plastic, burnt through fabric and control panels, and filled up the engines and cockpits, even tipping some of the aircraft on their tails with the sheer weight of ash and pumice. Lava flowed down the sides of the mountain threatening the aircraft base and the towns of San Sebastiano, Massa di Somma and Ottaviano, as well as part of San Giorgio a Cremano. On 22 March the aircraft base was evacuated.

Dr Leander K. Powers, a captain in the Medical Corps. who was stationed in Italy, kept a diary and wrote 'Thursday morning (22nd March), we rode down beyond Pompeii. The cinders were so deep that traffic was stopped. Along about noon, the wind changed and the cinders began falling on Torre Annunziato. Everything had a coat of black, just like light snow. We rode up toward the Naples side on the Autostrade, and, as the wind was blowing toward town, I got a wonderful view of the boiling inferno. Yesterday, (21st March) I rode into the town that was destroyed by the flowing lava and apparently the flow was coming to a stop, but the devastation was terrific. Tonight there is a lot of lightning coming from the crater and infrequent blasts. I learned from an Allied Military Government officer that 78 planes (B-25) were destroyed on the Pompeii airfield during the past few days by the lava and cinders.'[3] By Friday 30 March the eruption was over.

Living in the shadows

Currently there is a population of approximately two million people living in the shadow of Vesuvius, a number which is regularly swelled to over three million by tourists. The Italian authorities do have an evacuation plan for the area and regular exercises by emergency services are carried out, but scientists who have been monitoring the mountain for many years are fearful that a cataclysmic eruption is on the cards.

22 The humpback volcano. The white specks at the base of Vesuvius show just how close people live today, despite the danger.

Seismic monitors are placed all over the mountain and are monitored almost hourly, while gas emissions are measured and watched.

Humans can do very little to combat the destructive power of the volcano but that has not stopped us from trying. In January 1973 a 1,600-metre fissure opened near the small fishing town of Vestmannaeyjar on the island of Heimaey in Iceland. A wall of lava erupted from the ground threatening to cut off the town from the harbour. Residents were evacuated and the local fire brigade set up pipes and fire hoses and poured over 5 million tonnes of sea water on the northern edge of the flow. For five months the firemen and a few remaining residents battled to save their town. They succeeded and the harbour was saved but, although there were no casualties, some 360 of the town's houses (nearly one third) were destroyed and 400 were damaged.

It should perhaps be remembered that, although lava is incredibly hot (between 550°C and 1400°C), it travels fairly slowly and can usually be outmanoeuvred and outrun. On the other hand the pyroclastic flows and surges which flowed through Pompeii sped through the cities at approximately 600 miles per hour.

On 24 June 1982 British Airways flight 9 inadvertently flew through a volcanic ash cloud while flying in Indonesian air space. Mount Galunggung, near Jakarta, had erupted, throwing tons of volcanic debris into the atmosphere. Both air traffic control and the crew of flight 9 were unaware of the situation until the British Airways 747 started to experience strange phenomena. The passenger cabin began to fill with smoke, causing cabin crew to suspect a fire on board, but a search for the cause proved fruitless. Meanwhile visibility, in the cockpit, was poor with the windows being hit by what the flight crew thought was hail. Looking outside, the flight crew and the passengers could see strange lightning together with a bluish glow which surrounded the plane (St Elmo's fire). The volcanic pumice and ash choked all four engines causing a complete shut down. With no engines the 747 began to plummet towards the earth, but with the drop in altitude the brave flight crew were able to restart the engines and land safely with no loss of life. As a direct result of this incident it was agreed that in future geologists and air traffic control, worldwide, would liaise on future eruptions.

Bernard Chouet

Scientists have not given up in their efforts to predict when a volcano will erupt and there have been some successes. In 1986 Swiss-born Bernard Chouet, originally an electrical engineer, looked at the seismic readings of a volcano just prior to its eruption and saw what no one else had seen, a resonating signal—something he called a 'long period event'. Seismic activity had always been monitored but usually it was the 'A' type signal, or sharp dramatic burst that usually related to the cracking of the rocks under pressure, that was thought to be the key. What Chouet was interested in was the 'B' type signal: a slow long wave that indicated a pressure build up in the magma chamber—a 'long period event'. A good analogy is the pumping of air into a balloon: every time the air is pumped in there is a pressure build-up, and if more air is pumped in and not released, eventually the balloon will pop.

In January 1993 Chouet warned scientists that Galeras, a Colombian volcano, would erupt when he saw 'long period event' signals on seismic readings. However US volcanologist Stanley Williams, who used gas emissions to read volcanoes, saw things differently and, believing that Galeras was safe, he led a party of scientists into the crater on 14 January 1993. Tragically Galeras erupted, killing nine of the party and severely injuring Williams. It was a hard lesson, but the world was now willing to listen to Chouet.

Chouet has been able to put his theories to the test more than once, predicting correctly on two occasions when Mount Redoubt (Alaska) would erupt. In 2000 the Chouet method was used by Mexican

23   Vesuvius looks quiet and benign. There is no hint of the power that is buried deep within.

authorities to correctly predict the eruption of Popocatépetl—'the smoking mountain'—in that country and almost 56,000 inhabitants were successfully evacuated days before an eruption. Nonetheless, it is not now a foregone conclusion that all eruptions can safely be predicted and, if inhabitants are evacuated and a volcano does not then erupt, people are less likely to listen a second time.

Even as recently as March 2010 Mount Eyjafjallajökull in Iceland managed to bring a large part of the world to a stop when it erupted, causing an almost complete grounding of all European aircraft. This was primarily due to worries about possible catastrophic engine failure. On 5 January 2012 a snow-topped Mount Etna (one could call it a relative of Mount Vesuvius) erupted, spewing a plume of ash 5,000 metres into the air; thus starting the year with a bang and reminding the world what an active volcano can do.

And what of Vesuvius? Scientists and laymen alike agree that it is not a matter of if, but when Vesuvius will erupt again, and it is thought that when she does, it is likely to be a big one.

Notes

1 **Baum, L. Frank** (under the pseudonym **Edith Van Dyne**), *Aunt Jane's Nieces Abroad*, chapter V:'Vesuvius Rampant',1906, quoted on

http://www.gutenberg.org/files/16566/16566-h/16566-h.htm#Page_54

2 **Cooley, Alison E.** and **Cooley, M.G.L.,** *Pompeii: A Source Book* (London: Routledge, 2004), p. 210.

3. **Powers, Dr Leander K.,** quoted at

http://www.warwingsart.com/12thAirForce/Vesuvius.html

Living in the shadows

Since everything will be destroyed in this way, what kind of people ought you to be? You ought to live holy and godly lives as you look forward to the day of God and speed its coming. That day will bring about the destruction of the heavens by fire, and the elements will melt in the heat. But in keeping with his promise we are looking forward to a new heaven and a new earth, the home of righteousness. So then, dear friends, since you are looking forward to this, make every effort to be found spotless, blameless and at peace with him. Bear in mind that our Lord's patience means salvation, just as our dear brother Paul also wrote you with the wisdom that God gave him.

2 Peter 3:11–15

M any parallels have been drawn between the cities of Pompeii and Herculaneum and those of Sodom and Gomorrah, two biblical cities so wicked that God wiped them from the face of the earth: 'Then the Lord rained down burning sulphur on Sodom and Gomorrah' (Genesis 19:24). The similarities, it seems, were not lost on others, as someone had written 'Sodom and Gomorrah' on the walls of a house on the corner of Via dell'Abbondanza.

Whether the words were written by a citizen of the doomed city or subsequently by someone involved in the recovery there is little doubt that the Roman way of life was immoral, idolatrous, cruel and barbaric and the eventual downfall of the Roman Empire, like that of other ancient super powers, was predicted in the Bible (Daniel chapters 2 and 7). But is the world we live in today really much different to those mentioned above?

A world of discoveries

The twenty-first century is an amazing place in which new discoveries are

24 The restored version of John Martin's Destruction of Pompeii and Herculaneum.

made on an almost daily basis, and seems very far removed from that of AD 79. We in the West have every modern comfort and convenience at our fingertips; medicine has advanced to an extent that the average life expectancy exceeds our 'seventy years, or eighty, if our strength endures' (Psalm 90:10). We have gone boldly where no man has gone before; pushing our boundaries to the moon and, by unmanned vehicle, to Mars and by space probes to the very edges of our solar system, while modern means of communication and the World Wide Web have conquered the globe in a way the Romans never could. However, upon closer examination we can see many parallels between today's modern civilisation and that of ancient Pompeii after all: even though the outward circumstances of life change dramatically, the heart and nature of man is always the same. As great progress is made in science and technology, the generation in which we live endeavours more and more to reject the one true Creator God in favour of a multitude of idols, be they science, money, fame, pop stars, film stars, sporting heroes, or perhaps worst of all the 'I'll do it my way' mentality that is so prevalent today.

The persecution of Christians continues even today. In England, which many still think of as 'a Christian country', we see the cultural appreciation of the gospel being eroded. Laws are being passed that are slowly restricting the freedom of Christians in this land. In other parts of the world it is not unusual for churches to be closed, pastors to be thrown into jail and for people to be tortured or even killed for their faith. Having said these things, we should not be surprised for Christ himself said that 'If they persecuted me, they will persecute you also' (John 15:20).

An uncaring world

The 'end of the world' scenario is now a common feature of television documentaries and science fiction films. There is little doubt that we are living in the last days, a period initiated by Jesus' first coming and due to end when he comes again, but many people seem obsessed with the idea of trying to predict when that last day will be; a foolhardy and, dare I say it, arrogant attempt to know what Jesus himself did not know while he walked this earth ('No one knows about that day or hour, not even the angels in heaven, nor the Son, but only the Father' Matthew 24:36). The people of Pompeii were very superstitious and they too liked to predict the future, but they were totally unprepared for what happened. We also live surrounded by people who seem unaware or uncaring of the dangerous situation they are in.

Instead of challenging us to use our mathematical, scientific or Biblical skills to calculate the time when this world will reach its climax in the return of Christ, the Bible encourages us instead to simply be prepared for when it does come. It is clear from the New Testament that the early Christians lived with a sense of the imminence of Christ's return even though they knew that it would be like a man returning from a distant country (Luke 19:12–14) and that the date could not possibly be anticipated (1 Thessalonians 5:1). In reflecting on the tragic events of Pompeii and Herculaneum I believe that the most important thing we can learn from the fate of the people of is that we should be prepared to meet God—either at his coming in glory or in our death before that great event takes place.

The Bible makes it clear that the only way to be sure that we are ready is to come to God to repent of our sins and to put our faith and trust in Christ's atoning sacrifice as our hope of heaven.

The well-known preacher Charles Haddon Spurgeon (1834–1892), who visited the ruins in December 1871, echoed this sentiment when he wrote:

'In the ear of our imagination have sounded voices from the dead in Pompeii, and in a hurried moment we sit down to record the impressions they have made.

'The full chorus of the disinterred chants one solemn line, "Be ye also ready, for in such an hour as ye think not the Son of Man cometh." To many in that fair abode of luxury and vice the outbreak of Vesuvius appeared to be the end of all things. When the darkness might be felt settled down upon them; when the earth rumbled and reeled beneath them; when the groaning waves of the tortured sea foamed beyond them; when the scorching glare of vivid lightnings flashed above them, and huge rocks blazing and hissing with fire fell all around them; they believed that the world's death had come,—and so, indeed, in a manner it had come to them, but in a fuller and truer sense it hastens on for us! Even now, while the ink is flowing from our pen, the Lord may be on his way, and may suddenly appear. In Pompeii's last tremendous hour the bread was in the oven, but the baker never saw it taken from it; the meat was seething in the pot never to be eaten; the slave was at the mill, the prisoner in the dungeon, the traveller at the inn, the money dealer in his treasury, but none of these saw aught of their labours, their pains, their pleasures, or their profits again. The burning dust fell over all, the poisonous vapours sought out every crevice, and the ocean of mud buried inhabitant and habitation, worshipper and temple, worker and all that he had wrought! Should a sudden overthrow come upon us also, are we ready? Could we welcome the descending Lord, and feel that for us his coming with clouds to recompense justice would be a joyful appearing, to be welcomed with exulting acclamation? The question is too important to be dismissed until honestly answered may sincerity direct the examination it suggests.'[1]

The Bible makes it clear that the only way to be sure that we are ready is to come to God, to repent of our sins and to put our faith and trust in Christ's atoning sacrifice as our hope of heaven.

Everything goes on as before

In the apostle Peter's second letter to his fellow believers, scattered due to persecution, he writes 'In the last days scoffers will come … They will say "Where is this 'coming' he promised? Ever since our fathers died, everything goes on as it has since the beginning of creation"' (2 Peter 3:3–4). To the people of Pompeii before the eruption it must have seemed very much that way. They had forgotten that just a few miles away, looking down upon them, was a silent but active volcano. Covered in grass, probably up to its crater, it seemed benevolent and benign. We too can take this world's continuing for granted and forget that the since the fall of man in the Garden of Eden, the 'whole creation has been groaning as in the pains of childbirth' (Romans 8:22) awaiting Christ's second coming.

Terrible events do occur, whether man-made disasters such as the sinking of the Titanic in 1912 or the destruction of the twin towers in New York in 2001, or natural catastrophes as the tsunami that struck Japan in 2011 and the destruction of Pompeii in AD 79. Like the Romans, we hold our breath for a moment; we wonder and question our existence, our frailty and even whether there is a God, but as time rolls on and days become months and months become years and we forget. We forget that 'today' could so easily be the last day.

What the Bible says

The Bible very clearly tells us that God's time is not our time for 'With the Lord a day is like a thousand years, and a thousand years are like a day' (2 Peter 3:8) and we are even told the reason for his delay 'He is patient with you, not wanting anyone to perish, but everyone to come to repentance' (2 Peter 3:9). But we are also told that 'The Lord is faithful to all his promises' (Psalm 145:13) so why should we doubt when Jesus tells us 'Be on guard! Be alert! You do not know when that time will come' (Mark 13:33).

Perhaps the only thing we can know for sure is how the world will end, and just as for the people of Pompeii it will end in fire 'The heavens will disappear with a roar; the elements will be destroyed by fire, and the earth and everything in it will be laid bare' (2 Peter 3:10).

What should we be doing?

So in the light of all that has been said, how should we then be living? Those who are not yet Christians need to realise that they are at enmity with God, 'for all have sinned and fall short of the glory of God' (Romans 3:23). The pleasant, comfortable lives we lead are merely the holding cells for inevitable judgement. Every day is spent in the shadow of a Holy God who will one day judge us for our sins. We need to turn to him, recognising our need of a saviour, realising that it is only through Jesus' sacrifice on the cross that we may approach God and that we need to do it now. 'Seek the Lord while he may be found' (Isaiah 55:6).

Drusilla and her son heard the message of the gospel from Paul, probably on more than one occasion. They listened to Paul preach 'on righteousness, self-control and the judgment to come' (Acts 24:24–25), and although we are told that her husband Felix was afraid, we are not told of her reaction. It is more than likely that she took no notice of the words preached to her.

If we are Christians then the scriptures very clearly tell us we need to be proactive in our response. We should be 'all the more eager to make [our] calling and election sure' (2 Peter 1:10). He does not mean that our election (salvation) is in any doubt if we have put our faith and trust in the Lord Jesus Christ. Christ himself says 'no-one can snatch them out of my hand' (John 10:28). No, it means that we must not give up, but continue holding fast to that faith and seeking to obey the Lord's commandments to the best of the abilities he has given us.

Running the race

When I was in my early twenties I worked in a well-known national sports centre, where regular athletic events were held. The apostle Paul, in many of his allegories, compared the Christian life with running a race, but in all of his comparisons never once does he say 'now you've been chosen by God, just sit back and relax'. The athletes who have been chosen to run in the final race do not just go to the starting blocks and sit down; they warm up, prime themselves and focus on the task before them; then they exert their utmost efforts in the running of the race, with eyes fixed firmly on the tape ahead. So, as Paul says, we should be 'forgetting what is behind and straining towards what is ahead ... press on towards the goal to win the prize for which God has called [us] heavenwards in Christ Jesus' (Philippians 3:13–14). We need to 'run with perseverance the race marked out for us' (Hebrews 12:1), for, unlike an athletics race, we can have more than one winner and, unlike the gold medal that they win, our prize will be eternal.

You can't take it with you

We also need to get our priorities right; 'for we brought nothing into the world, and we can take nothing out of it' (1 Timothy 6:7). When the

25 Bronze running statues from the Villa of Papyri.

people of Pompeii and Herculaneum fled they tried to carry their belongings or wealth and were caught by the destructive wave that erupted from Vesuvius. Their treasures and their gods could not save them, nor could they take their things with them into the afterlife. What do we hold on to in this world? Money, our homes, our jobs, our friends or our family? Of course, there is nothing wrong with any of these things, and they are all God-given, but we cannot take them with us and neither can they save us. We need to make sure that what we carry with us is something that will last. 'Store up for yourselves treasures in heaven, where moth and rust do not destroy, and where thieves do not break in and steal' (Matthew 6:20).

Dark and light

I once saw a play which told the story of a man who stood by the edge of a bottomless chasm. He tried to warn the oncoming mass of humanity of the danger as they, in dribs and drabs, approached the rim of the precipice. Sometimes he had success and was joined in his quest, but the majority of the time the people did not listen to him and they fell off the stage to their doom. Told on a darkened stage with flashes of light to illuminate the actors it was a very moving and haunting depiction of what this world faces.

There should be within us therefore the desire to share the word of God with others. We should be the warning voice, a light shining in the darkness illuminating the way. 'Do everything without complaining or arguing, so that you may become blameless and pure, children of God without fault in a crooked and depraved generation, in which you shine like stars in the universe as you hold out the word of life' (Philippians 2:14–16).

Like the people of Pompeii, or the passengers on board the Titanic, we may have to meet our maker long before Jesus comes again. We don't need to strap a pillow to our heads or trust in a life vest, hoping that it will protect us from the wrath to come. If we have made that step and become Christians we already have a 'shield'—our Lord and Saviour, Jesus Christ. However, we should not be lazy in our assurance. 'For this reason, make every effort to add to your faith goodness; and to goodness knowledge; and to knowledge, self-control; and to self-control, perseverance; and to perseverance, godliness; and to godliness, brotherly kindness; and to brotherly kindness, love.' (2 Peter 1:5–7). This is not intended to be a tick list, but an ongoing thing; we are all a 'work in progress' until the day Christ calls us into heaven.

Today is the day

When do we need to do all this? In Hebrews 3:7–8 and Psalm 95:7–8 it says 'Today, if you hear his voice do not harden your hearts' and in Hebrews 3:13 'encourage one another daily, as long as it is called today'. Today is the day. We are living in an extended period of grace, so we should not squander the opportunity that God has given us. Today is the day to put your faith and trust in the Lord Jesus Christ and seek his forgiveness, if you are not already his. Today is the day to put your life back on that narrow path with him; today is the day to seek one another's forgiveness; and today is the day we should tell someone else about the wrath of God that is to come and about the only one who can save us, for today is the last day for someone!

One day this world will come to an end and it will come when we least expect it, like 'a thief in the night' (1 Thessalonians 5:2). Perhaps for you it may not be a global event—maybe it will be just the end of your time.

Notes

1 http://www.spurgeon.org/s and t/voicesfp.htm

26   Another victim of the eruption; a man his head buried in his hands sits and awaits his fate.

A day at Pompeii

The following are just some of the buildings, etc., you may wish to visit on the archaeological site at Pompeii, the numbers in brackets are the numbers designated to them by Fiorelli and continued by subsequent archaeologists but they do give a guide to their location. It is important to remember that Pompeii is large and it is virtually impossible to see everything that there is to see in one day. Not all buildings are available to the general public, sometimes due to previous damage caused by tourists or a lack of funds to keep them open.

There is also only one public convenience on the site, which is located in the self-service restaurant near the Forum, so plan ahead! It can be very hot and dusty in Pompeii, so a hat, bottle of water, comfortable shoes and a map are a must.

You will hear a lot about 'styles' in respect to the murals found at Pompeii and Herculaneum. This refers to the time bracket they fall into—the 'first style' being the oldest dating back to about 200BC and the 'fourth style' being the youngest dating to around the time of the AD79 eruption.

Suburban Baths

Just before entering through the main entrance gate, on the left hand side are the remains of the Suburban Baths. Badly damaged in the earthquake of 62AD it was thought to have been 'closed for repair' at the time of the eruption. It has only recently been fully excavated.

Marine or Marina Gate (VII)

The Marine Gate, which is at the Western end of the Via

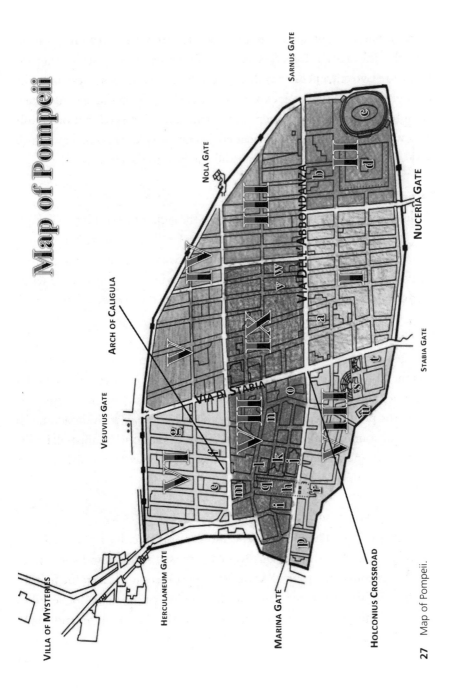

Map of Pompeii

VILLA OF MYSTERIES

HERCULANEUM GATE

VESUVIUS GATE

ARCH OF CALIGULA

NOLA GATE

SARNUS GATE

VIA DELL'ABBONDANZA

NUCERIA GATE

VIA DI STABIA

STABIA GATE

MARINA GATE

HOLCONIUS CROSSROAD

27   Map of Pompeii.

dell'Abbondanza, would originally have led from the harbour but now, with the sea many kilometres away, it is the main entrance to the site. There are two entrances or archways on the gate; one for pedestrians and a wider one possibly for packhorses (the road up from the marine gate is thought to have been too steep for vehicles). It is believed that originally the gates would have been barricaded in some way and manned by guards who controlled the flow of people and traffic into the city.

Temple of Venus (VIII–1–5) p

Slightly up from the Marine Gate and to the right once stood the Temple of Venus, the goddess of love, beauty and fertility. Unfortunately, very little remains of what was believed to have been a very beautiful temple. Heavily ransacked by treasure seekers, following the eruption the white marble would probably have been visible above the lava deposits.

The Forum (VII–8) h

A large rectangular square measuring 142m by 37m (466 by 124 feet), this was the heart of the community. Surrounded by porticoes on three sides and lined with temples, commercial and political buildings this was where the populace came to trade, worship and speak with the duumviri (the local councillors). Originally paved, it was seriously damaged by the earthquake and although repair work had begun it was not finished at the time of the eruption.

TEMPLE OF APOLLO (VII–7–32) l

Thought to have been one of the more popular cults in Pompeii the Temple of Apollo (the god of prophecy, music, healing and sometimes the Sun) is connected to the Forum by 11 entrances it has a statue to both Apollo and his twin sister Artemis (the goddess of the hunt). Believed to have been highly decorated with scenes of the Trojan War and many statues, it was heavily looted after the eruption.

BUILDING OF EUMACHIA (VII–9–1) J

There is some debate as to the original use of this building; whether it was used as the headquarters of the Fuller's Guild (fabric manufacturers, dyers and washers) or perhaps as a slave market. Built to honour the name of Eumachia, a local priestess, it also contained a life-size statue of the priestess as well as a statue honouring Empress Livia (Augustus' wife). At it's entrance you can still see the marble frieze, carved with birds, insects and snakes.

TEMPLE OF VESPASIAN (VII–9–2) K

Built after the earthquake, to venerate Emperor Vespasian who had contributed towards repairs. Believed to have been completely covered in white marble it would have been very impressive, but unfortunately there is very little trace of it left. In the centre of the temple is an altar depicting the sacrifice of a bull.

TEMPLE OF JUPITER (VIII–8–1) Q

Jupiter was chief of the Roman gods (as Zeus was to the Greeks). Dominating the north side of the Forum, the temple had two triumphal arches. Surrounded by columns, the rectangular temple has a stepped podium upon which was a large sacrificial altar.

MACELLUM (VII-7–7/8) L

A fish and meat market. The main entrance consisted of a room with two marble covered pedestals, on which may have stood statues. It was thought to have been made up of little shops with a large central fountain where the meat and fish could have been cleaned, with a marble gutter for carrying away the waste. Wall murals are still visible in some areas and displayed in two glass cases are the remains of some of Pompeii's victims.

28 The basilica: the law courts of the day.

The Basilica (VIII–1) r

Located on the west side of the Forum, the Basilica was the place where justice was administered and business was conducted. It was a large two storey building with three entrances opening onto a large hall with colonnades. It is thought to be one of the oldest surviving Roman buildings of its kind.

The Forum Baths (VII–5) m

The Forum Baths are believed to have been the only public baths fully operational at the time of the eruption. Surrounded by shops and 'takeaways' one can't help but be impressed by it. The domed changing rooms with its plaster covered niches, a gymnasium, a plunge pool in the Frigidarium and a large labrum (basin) in the Caldarium. The baths had everything necessary for the Roman way of life.

Arch of Caligula

Stands at the beginning of the Via di Mercurio. The large slit-like openings are thought to have once contained supports for statues of the Emperor Caligula.

House of the Tragic Poet (VI–8–3) e

Although not a large house it is very typical of the average home of that time. Named after a mosaic showing actors preparing to perform, it is perhaps more famous for its mosaic stating 'Beware of the Dog' in the main entrance. It was also the inspiration for the Pompeii Court at the Crystal Palace Exhibition and was used by Edward Bulwer-Lytton in his epic 'Last Days of Pompeii' as the house of Glaucus.

House of the Faun (VI–12–2) f

Named after the bronze statue discovered whilst excavating, unfortunately the one located on a pedestal in the middle of the

29 Doormat to the House of the Tragic Poet: Cave Canem ('beware of the dog').

impluvium is a copy, the original now being in the Naples Museum. It is the largest excavated house in Pompeii, entranced through an impressive columned doorway with a mosaic 'Welcome' doormat. It also boasted an impressive mosaic showing Alexander the Great fighting Darius at the Battle of Issus, which is now housed in the Naples Museum. An example of the 'first style' of decoration

House of the Vetti (VI–15–1) g

Probably owned by the rich Vetti brothers it is perhaps one of the most amazingly decorated houses in Pompeii with its many 'fourth style' murals of cherubs and stories of Greek mythology. It is also one of the busiest and most frequently visited houses on the site.

The Brothel (VII–12–18) n

The Lupanar, named after the howl of the she wolf, is made up of ten very small basic rooms over two floors with very uncomfortable looking stone beds, together with a small latrine. Covered in graffiti (fortunately in Latin) relating to the sexual prowess of the customers and the services offered by the unfortunates that worked there, it is also decorated in extremely crude paintings which leave very little to the imagination— you have been warned!!

Stabian Baths (VII–1–8) o

The largest of the bathing complexes in Pompeii. The main entrance on the Via Dell'Abbondanza leads into a large colonnaded Peristyle which would have been used as a gymnasium in its day. Some of the entrances to the baths had to be walled up after the earthquake as they became unsafe. On the right hand side would have been a swimming pool and on the left would have been the various temperature rooms, separated for men and women. Straight ahead would have been the latrine.

The Holconius Crossroads

Situated between the Via dell'Abbondanza and Via di Stabia, it would have been one of the busiest crossroads in its day. There is a large public fountain with a spout shaped like the head of a woman, which would have spewed forth its contents into a large square basin.

With your back to the Stabian Baths you will see that opposite is a thermopolium a 'fast food' joint, one of over 100 in Pompeii, the stone counter has holes in it which would have held large terracotta jars of hot or cold food. In the complex behind the thermopolium was the house where the inscription 'Sodom and Gomorrah' was discovered, unfortunately the inscription has long since disappeared and access may not be possible.

30   The Large Theatre. You can just about make out what is left of the porches on the stage.

Large Theatre (VIII–1.8) s

The seating area was arranged in terraces, with the most important spectators seated on specially raised platforms either side of the stage. The semi circle in the middle of auditorium would have been for the orchestra. The stage at the front was arranged with small porches which are thought to have housed statues. Audiences of up to 5,000 people would have watched the latest play be it a comedy or a tragedy.

Small Theatre (Odeon) (VIII–7–19) t

The theatrum tectum, or roofed theatre, would have housed 1,500 spectators and is thought to have put on music concerts or poetry recitals.

Temple of Isis (VIII–7–28) u

Deemed a bit of an oddity because it was dedicated to the Egyptian goddess of magic and rebirth, it was badly damaged in the earthquake of AD62. Thanks to an inscription found on the site we know that it was rebuilt, before the eruption, with funds given in the name of Numerius Popidius Celsinus who was only six years old at the time.

The Fullery of Stephanus (I–6–7) a

Originally a house, it is believed to have been converted following the earthquake and is an extremely well preserved fullery or laundry. In the main entrance its impluvium has been converted into a washing vat, and there are several other stone vats which were also used in the washing of the clothes; often substances like soda and animal urine were used in the cleaning process. The clothes were then dried on the upper terraces or on its special flat roof. At the time of the eruption the door of the laundry was barred shut and this door has been preserved by plaster cast and placed inside the building.

The House of the Chaste Lovers (IX–12–6) v

So named after the 'third style' fresco discovered showing a banqueting scene in which a couple can be seen kissing. On the North side of the building were discovered decorators tools and paints, left behind as their owners hurriedly made their exit.

The House of Polybius (IX–13–3) w

Named after a large number of political papers naming Julius Polybius which were found on site. It is a very impressive house and it was on this site that a number of skeletons were found including that of an eighteen year old pregnant girl, the remains of a foetal skeleton were recovered from within the girls abdomen.

The Nocera or Nuceria Gate

It is believed that the road entering through this gate was lowered at some time in order to make it less steep. Just west of the gate inside the city is the area known as 'The garden of fugitives' so called because a number of plaster cast bodies have been found. If you go through the gate you will find yourself in the Necropolis, or cemetery, where once a year a nine day festival of the dead was held and where families held picnics amongst the tombstones.

31 The Garden of Fugitives.

House of Venus in the Sea shell (II–3–3) p

This house was badly damaged during the World War II bombings but has been restored to something of its former grandeur. Named after a 'fourth style' painting which was uncovered on the back wall of the peristyle, it depicts Venus, goddess of love, lying on a sea shell flanked by two cherubs and a dolphin. The goddess' hair is particularly interesting as it shows the classic hairstyle popular during the reign of Nero.

The Amphitheatre (II–6) c

Although now overgrown with grass it is still definitely worth the long walk in order to view it. The scene of a riot in AD59, it is thought to be one of the oldest buildings designed specifically for gladiatorial games.

The Palestra (II–7) d

Next door to the Amphitheatre, this pedestrian only public space was used mostly by the male youth of the town as a gymnasium. Measuring

141 by 107 metres and rectangular in shape it has a 34 by 22 metre swimming pool in the middle, which at its deepest point, would have been 2.5 metres deep. You can get quite a good view of it from the top of the Amphitheatre.

Villa of Mysteries

Located outside of the city walls. You can exit through the Villa but not re-enter Pompeii, so you may want to make this the last stop. It is probably one of the best preserved villas on site. It is named after a 'second style' painting in the drawing room depicting a sort of Dionysian initiation ceremony, but experts cannot agree as to the sequence or depiction—hence the mystery! The villa is believed to have been sold after the earthquake and was gradually being converted into a vinery.

32 Via dell'Abbondanza. Note the stepping stones!

Timeline

753 BC   Supposed founding of Rome by Romulus.

73 BC   Slave revolt, led by Spartacus, who takes refuge at one point in the crater of Mount Vesuvius.

55 BC   Julius Caesar tries to invade Britain—he was unsuccessful.

54 BC   Julius Caesar successful in invading Britain, but it was a short-term campaign and after only a few months the entire Roman army withdraw.

48 BC   Julius Caesar goes to Egypt where he meets Cleopatra.

45 BC   Caesar crowned 'Dictator for Life'.

44 BC   Julius Caesar murdered as he visits the Senate. Gaius Octavius Thurinus Augustus becomes Emperor Augustus.

4 BC   Possible date for the birth of Christ.

AD 14   Emperor Augustus dies and is succeeded by Emperor Tiberius.

AD 26   Pontius Pilate appointed prefect of Judea.

AD 28   Scholars believe John the Baptist was beheaded.

AD 32–36 Possible time of the crucifixion of Jesus.

AD 37   Death of Emperor Tiberius; he is succeeded by Caligula.

AD 41   Emperor Caligula assassinated; Claudius hailed as the new Caesar.

AD 43   Emperor Claudius successfully re-invades Britain.

AD 44   Jerusalem comes under the direct rule of Rome.

AD 47   Roman town of Colchester believed to have been established.

AD 54   Death of Claudius and succession of Nero.

AD 59   A riot breaks out in Pompeii's amphitheatre resulting in a ten-year ban on gladiatorial games.

AD 60–62 Boudicca, a leader of the British Iceni tribe, leads a revolt against the Romans but fails and ultimately commits suicide.

AD 62   A large earthquake thought to measure between 5 and 7 on the Richter Scale hits the region of Campania with Pompeii at its epicentre.

Scholars believe that the apostle Paul was held under house arrest in Rome.

AD 64   Nero supposedly fiddled while Rome burned, Christians blamed for starting the fire and their persecution begins.

Popular belief has the apostle Peter crucified upside-down.

In Jerusalem the third Great Temple is finished after 84 years of construction.

AD 65   Scholars believe that the Gospel of Mark was written during this year.

AD 66   Gessus Florus, Roman Procurator of Judea allows massacre of Jews in Ceasaera, Jewish zealots attack Roman garrison and seize control of the fortress at Masada.

AD 67   Roman armies under Titus Flavius Sabinus Vespasianus puts down zealot revolt. Jewish General Joseph Ben Matthias holds out in Jotapta but later surrenders.

33 The Herculaneum boat sheds. Originally on the seafront, many of the people thought they would be safe by taking shelter there. Undiscovered till 1981, which gave rise to the belief that most of the citizens of Herculaneum had survived the eruption.

Scholars believe that the Apostle Paul was executed during this year, beheaded.

AD 68 Roman senate sentences Nero to death, but he flees only to commit suicide. Servius Sulpicius Galba rules for six months.

History of the Jewish People was written by General Joseph Ben Matthias—who has now adopted a Roman name Flavius Josephus.

AD 69 Galba murdered by Marcus Salvius Otho who then was recognised by the Senate as emperor. Three months later he commits suicide after losing a battle with rival Vitellius (who in turn was killed by Vespasian's army).

AD 70 Vespasianus lays siege to Jerusalem but returns to Rome leaving his son Titus to continue with the help of Herod Agrippa II of Chalais. Jerusalem falls and most of the third temple is destroyed, leaving only the 'Wailing Wall'.

Vespasian becomes emperor.

AD 73 Roman forces finally battle their way into the Jewish fortress of Masada, but only two women and five children are left alive, the rest having committed suicide.

Work begins on the Colosseum.

A chronological table of events

AD 75	The town of Chester in England is believed to have been founded.
AD 79	Emperor Vespasian dies and is succeeded by his son Titus.
	'Histori a Naturalis' is published by Pliny the Elder, a 37-volume encyclopaedia of natural history.
	Eruption of Mount Vesuvius.
1689	Identification of La Civita as Pompeii.
1709	Accidental discovery of Herculaneum.
1860	Giuseppe Fiorelli becomes inspector of the excavations and institutes the systematic numbering of all streets and houses.
1863	Fiorelli begins to plaster cast the hollows left by the decaying dead.
1944	Most recent eruption of Vesuvius.
1981	Discovery of bodies at Herculaneum inside shelters at what was once the seafront, confirming that the population did not all escape.
1997	Pompeii and Herculaneum declared UNESCO world heritage site.
2010	Gladiatorial school collapses due to erosion and neglect, this is followed by the collapse of the House of the Moralist. UNESCO sends in a team of experts to investigate the state of Pompeii's conservation.
2011	Sewer and septic tank at Herculaneum opened to archaeologists.
	UNESCO and Italy agree to co-operate on restoration of Pompeii.

Glossary

Aedile: a local magistrate, elected annually, who had the charge of public buildings, games, markets, police etc.

Atrium: the entrance hall or chief apartment of a Roman house

Basilica: a large oblong hall with double colonnades and commonly a semi-circular apse used for judicial and commercial purposes

Caldarium: hot room of a Roman bath

Caldera: a large crater formed by the collapse of the central part of a volcano

Consul: the highest political office in the Republic and, although with no real political power, during the reign of the emperors, elected annually

Crater: bowl-like mouth of a volcano

Cubiculum: bedroom

Duumvir: one of two senior, annually elected, magistrates at Pompeii

forum: open square in a town, surrounded by public buildings, focus of religious, commercial, administration and judicial affairs

Freedman/Freedwoman: a male or female ex-slave

Frigidarium: cold room of a Roman bath

Hellenistic: Greek culture originating after the death of Alexander the Great (323 BC)

Herm: a head or bust on a square base

Hypocaust: Floors suspended on brick piles, that allow hot air to circulate and heat rooms (central heating system)

Ides: the thirteenth or fifteenth of the Roman month

Impluvium: a square basin in the atrium that received the rainwater from the open space in the roof

Laconicum: hot tub or sauna in a Roman bath

Lapilli: small fragments (in size from a pea to a walnut) of lava ejected from a volcano

Lararium: shrine for the household gods

Lava: molten material discharged in a stream from a volcano or fissure; such material subsequently solidified

Magma: a pasty or doughy mass of organic or mineral material; molten or pasty rock material

Glossary of Terms

Necropolis: a cemetery or burial site

Palaestra: large open area, surrounded by a colonnade, for exercise

Pax Romana: Roman Peace

Peristylum: a range of columns round a square garden

Proconsul: a Roman magistrate with almost consular authority outside the city

Procurator: a financial agent in, or an administrator of, a Roman imperial province

Pumice: an acid glassy lava so full of gas cavities that it floats in water; light rock ejected from a volcano

Pyroclastic flow: a flow of rocks, ash, dust and debris ejected from a volcano that cascades down the side of a volcano reaching high temperature and speeds

Pyroclastic surge: a fluidised mass of turbulent gas and rock fragments which flows down the side of a volcano reaching high temperature and speeds

Quiescent period: resting or inactive period of time

St Elmo's Fire: an electrical charge forming a bright blue or violet glow around a church spire, ships mast, etc.

Senate: the ruling council of Rome

Tepidarium: warm room of a Roman bath

UNESCO: United Nations Educational, Scientific and Cultural Organisation

Vestal Virgin: a virgin girl of noble birth consecrated to Vesta (goddess of hearth and household) who kept the sacred fire burning on the altar

Volcanology: the scientific study of volcanoes and volcanic phenomena

Select Bibliography

Beard, Mary, *Pompeii, The Life of a Roman Town* (London: Profile Books Ltd, 2008)

Bentley, Michael, *Living for Christ in a Pagan World* (Co. Durham: Evangelical Press, 1990)

Cooley, Alison E. and **Cooley, M.G.L.,** *Pompeii: A Source Book* (London: Routledge, 2004)

Dickens, Charles, *Pictures from Italy* (Fairfield, Iowa: 1st World Library—Literary Society, 2004)

Hicks, Peter, *Pompeii and Herculaneum (Digging Up The Past)* (Hove: Wayland Publishers Ltd, 1995)

Ling, Roger, *Pompeii: History, Life and Afterlife* (Gloucestershire: Tempus Publishing Limited, 2005)

Nappo, Salvatore, *Pompeii: A Guide to the Ancient City* (London: Weidenfeld & Nicolson, 1998)

Twain, Mark, *The Innocents Abroad* (Hertfordshire: Wordsworth Editions Limited, 2010)

Wilkinson, Paul, *Pompeii: The Last Day* (London: B BC Books, B BC Worldwide Ltd, 2003)

Wallace-Hadrill, Andrew, *Houses and Society in Pompeii and Herculaneum* (Chichester, West Sussex: Princeton University Press, 1994)

Useful websites

http://sites.google.com/site/ad79eruption

http://oplontisproject.org

Picture and photograph credits

All images have been sourced from WikiPedia Commons (http://commons.wikimedia.org). A search on the filenames will give the full details of the image.